What Others Say About 'SPARKS OF SPIRIT'

"Having always led a successful and productive life, I was very angry, confused, and depressed when I hit a very difficult and frustrating period. The profound writings in your book, Sparks of Spirit, were a daily source of inspiration to me and one of the mainstays that led me out of the darkness and back into the light. I knew that God was teaching me lessons, and your book constantly reminded me of His metaphysical wisdom and love. There was and is a reason for everything."

—**Linnda Durré, Ph.D., psychotherapist, author, motivational speaker & TV/Radio Talk Show Host**

"In Sparks of Spirit, your thoughts, The Four Noble Truths and the Eightfold Path meet Torah and the Beatitudes—also a little Black Elk and echoes of the reverent religion of the Great Mother of antiquity (and now). You go deeply into your own specific tradition and through its integrity you encounter the universal experience of holiness and mystery."

—**The Rev. Alla Renée Bozarth, Ph.D. author of *At the Foot of the Mountain* and *All Shall Be Well, All Shall Be One***

"I asked one of our discreet priests to read the Sparks of Spirit manuscript. He advises me that the material is very good and will help many people to relate to the God of Abraham, Isaac and Jacob. He found it good material for meditation and was enthusiastic about your ability to write."

—**Cardinal Timothy Manning, Archbishop of Los Angeles**

"*Your book, Sparks of Spirit, is inspirational, interestingly written, and contains many practical tools for developing and maintaining a useful and happy life.*"

—**Dr. Norman Vincent Peale, Marble Collegiate Church, New York City, NY**

"*Many people are troubled these days, and they are searching for ways to find help. Sparks of Spirit may reach their needs and prove to be most helpful to them.*"

—**Rabbi Aaron M. Wise, Adat Ari El, North Hollywood, CA**

Sparks of Spirit

Books by Rolf Gompertz

Abraham, The Dreamer—An Erotic and Sacred Love Story
(Biblical novel)

A Jewish Novel About Jesus
(Biblical novel)

SPARKS OF SPIRIT
How to Find Love & Meaning in Your Life
(Personal Development Guide)

The Messiah of Midtown Park
(Play/Comedy-Drama)

A CELEBRATION OF LIFE
(Poetry and Prose)

For additional information, please see
About the Author/Books **at back of this book**

How to Obtain These Books

These books are available as paperbacks from the publisher's online book store at http://www.iUniverse.com or from http://www.amazon.com. The books may be inspected and browsed at either place before ordering. At the web site *select* the *book store* and *search* by *author's name* (Rolf Gompertz) or the particular *book title*. If a title has not been posted yet, it will be shortly. You may also contact the author for more information and updates. Mailto: rolfgompertz@yahoo.com.

Please address any correspondence with the author to:
P.O. Box 9761, North Hollywood, CA 91609
Telephone/fax: 1(818) 980-3576 E-mail: rolfgompertz@yahoo.com

Sparks of Spirit

❖

How to Find Love and Meaning in Your Life 24 Hours a Day

ROLF GOMPERTZ

Author of *Abraham, The Dreamer—An Erotic and Sacred Love Story* and *A Jewish Novel About Jesus*

To Sarah —
Bloom where you stand!
Love, Blessings & Shalom —
Rolf Gompertz

iUniverse, Inc.
New York Lincoln Shanghai

Sparks of Spirit
How to Find Love and Meaning in Your Life 24 Hours a Day

All Rights Reserved © 1983, 2004 by Rolf Gompertz

No part of this book may be reproduced or transmitted in any form or by any means, graphic, electronic, or mechanical, including photocopying, recording, taping, or by any information storage retrieval system, without the written permission of the publisher.

iUniverse, Inc.

For information address:
iUniverse, Inc.
2021 Pine Lake Road, Suite 100
Lincoln, NE 68512
www.iuniverse.com

Originally published as *Sparks of Spirit—How to Find Love and Meaning in Your Life 24 Hours a Day, From Now On*

First edition, 1983, The Word Doctor Publications,
Copyright © 1983 by Rolf Gompertz

Cover design by Menachem and iUniverse, Inc.
Author image by Debra Halberstadt, HalfCity Productions

Grateful acknowledgment is given for the use of biblical verses from *The Holy Scriptures, According to the Masoretic Text.* Copyright © 1917, 1955 (New Edition, fourth impression, 1965). Approved version of The Jewish Publication Society. Used by permission of the Jewish Publication Society.

ISBN: 0-595-30726-4

Printed in the United States of America

TO

CAROL

WHO ASKED

HOW

Contents

About This Book..xiii

Acknowledgments...xvii

CHAPTER 1	How to Find Love and Meaning in Your Life 24 Hours a Day	1
CHAPTER 2	How to Overcome That Lonely Feeling	5
CHAPTER 3	How to Think of God.....................	11
CHAPTER 4	How I Can Come to Feel God's Love	16
CHAPTER 5	How to Think of God's Ways	22
CHAPTER 6	How I Can Always Be Sure of Mercy from God	26
CHAPTER 7	How to Make All Things Work for You	30
CHAPTER 8	How to Overcome Fear.....................	34
CHAPTER 9	How to See Myself	37
CHAPTER 10	How I Don't Have to Worry about What Others Think, Say, or Do	39
CHAPTER 11	How I Can Become Confident of God's Personal Concern for Me............................	44
CHAPTER 12	God as Helper, or, How to Relax.............	50
CHAPTER 13	How to Be Happy........................	58
CHAPTER 14	How to Become Trusting	61
CHAPTER 15	How to Find Meaning in My Life............	65

Chapter 16	How to Develop a Right Attitude 71
Chapter 17	How I Can Become and Stay Healthy 81
Chapter 18	The Spiritual Laws of Life and How They Operate 84
Chapter 19	How to Feel Safe 92
Chapter 20	How I Can Find Peace....................96
Chapter 21	How I Can Be Abundant..................99
Chapter 22	How God Is Spirit 102
Chapter 23	How Life Is Symbol.....................105
Chapter 24	How to Do the Right Thing 108
Chapter 25	How I Am Looking for God and How God Is Looking for Me 113
Chapter 26	How I Can Change 119
Chapter 27	How to Stay Joyful......................123

About the Author 127
Other Books by Rolf Gompertz........................131

About This Book

Some time in the late 1960s my wife, Carol, challenged me, saying:

"It's very fine and good for you to have a spiritual outlook on life. But not everyone has one. How can others get one? How can they learn to see themselves and the world from a spiritual point of view?"

I was taken aback by the question. I didn't have an answer. But the question intrigued me and haunted me. That's how *Sparks of Spirit* came into being. It is my answer.

My wife is a very practical person. She does not like abstractions. She likes concrete information. She wants explanations that tell her and show her how to do something. She likes "how-to" books. So this is a "how-to" book. It is not the first, only, or final word on the matter. It is a spiritual First Aid kit.

The "system" is a very simple one. It is explained in the first chapter. It depends on the internalizing of phrases or verses that jump out at you and speak to you. Many of us are already doing this in other ways. We have favorite expressions that we live with. Some are words to live by, which we've picked up from fathers, mothers, grandparents; from friends or strangers; from secular or spiritual teachers; from secular or sacred authors. These are the "mantras" of our life, which we have picked up here and there, seemingly willy-nilly.

They work. They are a short-hand for volumes of words. We can keep mantras in our heads much more easily than long passages and texts. Short sayings come to our aid at a moment's notice, when we need to decide on attitudes and actions regarding serious matters.

To achieve or refine a *spiritual* point of view, you can build on what you are doing already. What I am offering is perhaps a more conscious, guided, systematic approach. The first chapter of this book explains the simple method. It tells you what to do and how to do it. It provides direction, but, at the same time allows you flexibility and freedom of choice. You do not measure your journey by time or distance. You proceed on inner time and over inner distance. It should be a joyful journey of ongoing spiritual discovery about yourself, others, the cosmos, and God.

This is a practical book. Each of the 27 chapters addresses a different topic, involving matters of personal concern, such as: How to Overcome That Lonely Feeling, How to Think of God, How I Can Come to Feel God's Love, How to Make All Things Work for You, How to Find Meaning in My Life, How to See Myself, How I Can Become Confident of God's Personal Concern for Me, How to Stay Joyful.

What, then, are the spiritual underpinnings on which *Sparks of Spirit* is based? I would call my outlook *practical mysticism*.

Sparks of Spirit is based on the belief that the universe, in essence, is a spiritual universe. The whole cosmos is spirit, manifesting in many forms; the whole universe is spirit, from sand grains to galaxies. We, human beings, live, and move and have our being in a spiritual universe; we are spiritual beings.

What then is the basic nature of the cosmos, from atom to Adam? We and everything we can observe are involved in a dynamic, reciprocal Love Process, consisting of *Giving and Receiving*, constantly, everywhere and at all times. *Giving and Receiving* is also another way of saying *Loving and Being Loved*. Giving and Receiving, Loving and Being Loved *describe* the dynamic, reciprocal Love Process.

The cosmic Love Process includes, but is much more than, what we ordinarily understand by human Love. The dynamic, reciprocal Love Process permeates the cosmos. It is the key that unlocks the nature of the universe, in all its awesome splendor and power.

This Love is also the very key to God, creator of the Cosmos. The cosmos is an expression of its Creator; since the cosmos is Love, God is Love. God is a God of Love, Giving and Receiving, Loving and Being Loved, in the Eternal Now, for all Eternity.

Love, therefore, is also basic to human beings, who have been created in the image of God. Love is the operative principle of our lives, and of life itself. We are here to love and learn to love. We are here to love and serve God, through the love and service of our fellow human beings. We can see everything we do in this light. What greater meaning, or greater reward, could our lives have?

Sparks of Spirit is about seeing things from this perspective; it is about learning what it means to love and to see life through the prism of love. *Sparks of Spirit* refers to truths frozen into words. As these sparks touch your spirit, they release their power within you, transforming your life, enriching it, and filling it with meaning and love, 24 hours a day.

Finally, sparks of spirit are more than truths frozen into words. We, ourselves, are sparks of spirit, sailing through the universe, stopping here and there for a momentary connection, but having only one permanent connection, the divine connection—our connection to a loving God, in whom we live and move and have our being.

May your journey be filled with light and peace, love and meaning, 24 hours a day, now and forever.

Rolf Gompertz
December 17, 2003

Acknowledgments

I wrote *Sparks of Spirit—How to Find Love and Meaning in Your Life 24 Hours a Day* in the late 1960s. I am grateful to my wife, Carol, who inspired it by her question about how to develop a spiritual outlook on life.

It was not until 1983 that *Sparks of Spirit* was published through my company, The Word Doctor Publications.

This, now, is a new edition. The basic text is the same. But the introduction, author biography, information about my other books, front and back cover design and content are new. So is the publisher, iUniverse, Inc.

The quoted endorsements are a mixture of original ones (Rabbi Aaron M. Wise, Dr. Norman Vincent Peale, Cardinal Timothy Manning) and new ones (The Rev. Alla Renée Bozarth, Ph.D., Linnda Durré, Ph.D.).

My deep thanks to them for their thoughtful comments, valuable quotes, and generosity of spirit.

Grateful acknowledgment is given for the use of passages from *The Holy Scriptures, According to the Masoretic Text*. Copyright © 1917, 1955 (New Edition, fourth impression, 1965). Approved version of The Jewish Publication Society. Used by permission of the Jewish Publication Society.

This book, as my other recent books, has been published according to a new publishing model, which I call Print-on-Demand Partnership Publishing (POD-PP). I am grateful to iUniverse, and similar publishers, for creating this new publishing model for authors, so that our books have a better chance to see the light of day and find their audiences. To those, at iUniverse, who have worked with me, my heartfelt thanks for your special skills, creative talents, constant caring and friendly, patient guidance.

1

How to Find Love and Meaning in Your Life 24 Hours a Day

You deserve to feel love and be loved.

You deserve to feel and know that you matter and that your life has meaning.

You deserve to feel that way, 24 hours a day, every day, for the rest of your life, from now on.

The good news is: you CAN feel that way.

And, if you are already feeling good about yourself and life, you can feel better.

I don't care who you are or what your circumstances—what you have gone through or what you are going through—I can help make your life happier and help you find love and meaning, every moment, for the rest of your life.

Does this sound too good to be true? It is not. I have proved it to myself in my own life.

"That's easy for you to say," you may tell me. "You don't have my problems!"

So, what problems are you talking about:

CAREER DISAPPOINTMENTS—A dead-end job? Work that seems meaningless? A sense of failure at mid-life? Having to settle for something less than you had hoped to achieve professionally?

PERSONAL DISAPPOINTMENTS—Feeling that you don't matter, that you are unimportant, that you are useless, that you are not needed, that you are unloved?

FAMILY TENSIONS—Problems with a spouse, children, other family members?

HEALTH PROBLEMS—Short-term, long-term? Yours or of those you love? Catastrophic illness? Expected or unexpected death?

MONEY MATTERS—Not being able to afford the things you'd like to have and do?

OUTLOOK ON LIFE—Feeling and being unhappy most of the time? Not getting much joy out of life? Feeling anxious and afraid? Wishing that you had a more easy-going, happy, cheerful disposition? Wishing you could get along better with others?

OK. So you are suffering from some or all of these problems and disappointments.

I have a surprise for you! I have suffered from just about every one of these, too. Really suffered!

I have another surprise for you! I have found a way to take that suffering and overcome it and change it, so that I can honestly say now that I have learned how to be happy and find love and meaning in my life 24 hours a day, for the rest of my life!

Furthermore, I also can help you be happy and find love and meaning in your life, 24 hours a day, for the rest of your life, from this moment on.

How? With *Sparks of Spirit*.

The technique and outlook are designed to help you achieve happiness, love and meaning in your life instantly, and on a long-term basis.

Even if you already have found good answers and techniques, my handbook for personal happiness will offer you a further source of confirmation, insight and inspiration.

Actually, there are all kinds of answers and techniques for coping with life. People drink to loosen up, to forget; they smoke, to relax and overcome fear; they overeat, to reward themselves, to overcome frustration, and as a substitute for love. People go from love affair to love affair to feel warm and loved and to overcome their sense of loneliness and aloneness. People acquire more and more material things, without ever feeling satisfied. People think that if they were richer or more successful or did more important things, life would be happier or more meaningful.

These are all answers and techniques but they don't work, they fall short of the mark, they are unfulfilling.

I found that a spiritual outlook works much better. It provides much more satisfactory ways of dealing with life and all our needs and problems.

I developed such an outlook. But how do you explain and teach a spiritual outlook? I figured out a simple system. I call it *practical mysticism*, with the emphasis on *practical*.

It doesn't matter what direction you are coming from: *Sparks of Spirit* will work for you.

It is non-denominational. It will work for you if you are Jewish or Christian, or if you belong to any other faith group. It is a bridge that can help you return to your religious roots, if that is what you are looking for, or it simply can provide you with another source of insight and inspiration, if you are already part of a spiritual community.

The book will also work for you if you are not comfortable with traditional religious beliefs or have never known such beliefs, yet are looking for a spiritual outlook on life.

If you have found Oriental mysticism and meditation attractive, you will find something here that will speak to you in Western terms.

Sparks of Spirit is a spiritual First Aid kit. When we hurt, we need help right away. When we are hungry, we need food right away. When we are thirsty, we need something to drink right away.

This book offers you instant help for whatever you need at any moment.

Simply select a topic, a chapter that speaks to your particular and immediate interest and need.

You can stay with that chapter, that topic one day, one week or even one month, as your need dictates. You may come back to that topic any time.

The particular chapter does not take long to read—three or four minutes at the most. But it goes to the heart of the matter. It should be read in the morning and in the evening. You should think about it, or even re-read it during the day.

In addition, each chapter, each topic is followed by a list of biblical verses that express the same idea. Truth, after all, is timeless and universal. You should pick one verse for each day, memorize it and live with it (put the verse on a 3x5 card and carry it around with you).

Sparks of Spirit are phrases and sentences which capture some aspect of truth. *Sparks of Spirit* are truth frozen into words.

These words spring to life upon contact. They will jump out at you, you will light up as you read them, as you hold on to them, as you dwell on them. Spirit answers spirit, soul speaks to soul, through the medium of language.

Once these sparks touch your spirit, they release their power within you and make you come alive with their truth.

A soldier goes through basic training to be equipped for battle. Many of us exercise, swim or jog, to stay in good physical condition.

The spirit, too, needs basic training. The soul, too, needs spiritual conditioning.

The mind must be occupied with something. We feed it daily with positive or negative matters. I hope that these *Sparks of Spirit* will have the power of conditioning you to act and react in such a way that you will make the most of life.

I know that this handbook for personal happiness can help you gain and maintain Love and Meaning in your life 24 hours a day—from now on!

2

How to Overcome That Lonely Feeling

We are individuals. There is no other human being exactly the same as you or I. This is the basis that gives profound meaning and profound concern to life.

To be unique means that every one of us is special. It means that no one else can fill our role. It truly means that God has assigned us a special mission. Each one of us, therefore, has meaning and importance in the eyes of God.

But there is a concern that accompanies our uniqueness. The fact that we are special also means that, essentially, we are different from any other human being. It means that we are separate. It means that we are alone.

We try to cover up our loneliness in many ways. We run from it by keeping busy, by mixing with people, by getting married and thus having someone around at all times to keep us company, by being surrounded by children and family, by belonging to organizations, by participating in group activities, by going along with the crowd in sports and politics.

But we can never escape our essential loneliness. It hits us sooner or later when others leave and the crowds are gone and the frantic pace of activity stops and we are turned inward upon ourselves.

Whichever way we run to escape we are eventually blocked and confronted by our loneliness and aloneness.

This is God's way of teaching us that we are directly dependent on Him, that we are directly responsible to Him, that we are directly related to Him, that we are directly embraced by and brought into union with Him.

Only by turning to God can we overcome our loneliness and aloneness.

There is good reason for this.

When we consider our desires honestly, we must admit that we desire understanding, certainty, security, attention, and love constantly, 24 hours a day.

All our activities are efforts in this direction. We are constantly striving to attain these ends and yet, as we hurry and scurry to achieve the good will of others, we are never really satisfied and we are often disappointed.

The closest we come to what we essentially desire—unconditional love—is family love between parents and children or between husband and wife. But even these relationships are often far from ideal. When they are ideal, even then they are not lasting because, ultimately, there comes separation through death.

Whatever way we turn, we are turned back upon ourselves. We meet our aloneness and our loneliness. We overcome these in God.

God alone is present wherever we are.

God alone is not subject to death.

God alone is with us 24 hours a day, every moment of the day.

God alone can thus offer us the total love, understanding, companionship, reassurance, certainty, and security that we crave.

God alone has a direct line to us, because we share in His spirit and we are created in His image.

God alone can close the gap of separation and alienation that we otherwise feel from all other created beings.

To walk with God is to walk in union and communion with the Source of our being. To walk with God is to be united with Him in spirit. To walk with God is never to feel alone again.

<u>Verses</u>

God is with you in all that you do. Genesis 21:22

◆ ◆ ◆

Behold, I am with you, and will keep you wherever you go. Genesis 28:15

◆ ◆ ◆

I will not leave you. Genesis 28:15

♦ ♦ ♦

Surely the Lord is in this place; and I knew it not. Genesis 28:16

♦ ♦ ♦

This is the gate of heaven. Genesis 28:17

♦ ♦ ♦

I am the Lord in the midst of the earth. Exodus 8:18

♦ ♦ ♦

My presence shall go with you, and I will give you rest. Exodus 33:14

♦ ♦ ♦

I will walk among you. Leviticus 26:12

♦ ♦ ♦

The Lord your God has been with you; you have lacked nothing. Deuteronomy 2:7

♦ ♦ ♦

The Lord your God is with you. Deuteronomy 20:1

◆ ◆ ◆

You are standing this day all of you before the Lord your God. Deuteronomy 29:9

◆ ◆ ◆

The Lord your God, He it is that does go with you. Deuteronomy 31:6

◆ ◆ ◆

I will not fail you, nor forsake you. Joshua 1:5

◆ ◆ ◆

The living God is among you. Joshua 3:10

◆ ◆ ◆

I have been with you wherever you didst go. II Samuel 7:9

◆ ◆ ◆

Holy, holy, holy, is the Lord of hosts; the whole earth is full of His glory. Isaiah 6:5

◆ ◆ ◆

Fear not, for I am with you. Isaiah 41:10

◆   ◆   ◆

The Lord will guide you continually. Isaiah 58:11

◆   ◆   ◆

You light my lamp. Psalm 18:29

◆   ◆   ◆

I will fear no evil, for You are with me. Psalm 23:4

◆   ◆   ◆

I will instruct you and teach you in the way, which you shall go. Psalm 32:8

◆   ◆   ◆

God is…a very present help in trouble. Psalm 46:2

◆   ◆   ◆

I am continually with you. Psalm 73:23

◆   ◆   ◆

Yours is the day, Yours also is the night. Psalm 74:16

♦ ♦ ♦

He that keeps you will not slumber. Psalm 121:3

♦ ♦ ♦

The eyes of the Lord are in every place. Proverb 15:3

3

How to Think of God

When we think of God, if we think of Him at all, we do so usually in some very limited way.

We think and speak of the God of Love or the God of Justice.

But the Bible speaks of God in many ways.

God is king, father, shepherd, savior, judge, creator, physician, provider.

God is a rock, an arm, a voice, a wing, a shield, a fortress, a fountain, a light.

God is justice, abundance, mercy, lovingkindness, compassion, graciousness, life, spirit, health, joy, peace, pleasantness.

The point is that we should think of God in accordance with our needs.

When we are concerned about health, we should think of God as the great physician and the source of health. We should identify with His health, which we share, being part of God.

When we are concerned about our mental powers, we should think of God as mind, knowing that we can attune our minds to His and receive some of His knowledge and wisdom.

When we need energy, we can think of God as the endless and abundant source of spiritual energy and we can open ourselves up to receive all we need from Him.

When we want life to be dependable, we can think of God as the law and lawgiver. We can think of the laws which He has built into the universe, and we can appreciate the order that exists in the universe, as we try to learn more about God's laws.

As we need protection, we can think of God as a shield sheltering us, or a parent holding us, or a fortress housing us.

Where, then, is God? Who is God? What is God?

Let us think of ourselves. There is our body and its various parts. But we are more than our body or the sum-total of its parts.

There is something central to that body, which we call the self, the soul. With it, the body is alive. Without it, the body is dead.

God and the universe can be understood in the same way. God is at the heart and center of the universe. The universe is God's body. God is more than the universe or the sum-total of its parts. God is the soul of that universe, God is that being at its center that gives it life, identity, direction and meaning.

Without God, the universe would be a dead universe. With God, the universe is eternally alive, because God is eternal.

Thus God and the universe are interlocked eternally. God's spirit is everywhere and in everything, flowing throughout many forms and levels of being that are in constant transformation.

Every being is part of God and God is part of every being. Every being has an awareness of God, and God is aware of every being. Every being can "talk" with God, and God can "talk" with every being.

Nothing is without God or God's spirit. The universe consists of an infinite variety of being, with infinite levels of awareness and consciousness, leading up to God, whose self-awareness is total, absolute, and real.

The words, the images are all meant to remind us of the many ways in which God is present in our life. The need of each moment dictates the image that will bring us into contact with God and that can help us hold Him in focus.

But we must remember that these are images only. They are audio-visual aids. They only talk about God—they are not God.

God, as He really is, is beyond human imaging. That's why, in a strict sense, there is a law, a commandment against making any kind of images of God.

God is spirit—that is the closest we can come in describing the indescribable.

The word "God" even is already saying too much, for God cannot be captured in words. God is beyond all symbols.

<u>Verses</u>

The Lord is a God of knowledge. I Samuel 2:3

◆   ◆   ◆

The Lord is my rock, and my fortress, and my deliverer. II Samuel 22:2

The Lord is my savior, You save me from violence.
II Samuel 22:3

♦ ♦ ♦

You are my lamp, O Lord. II Samuel 22:29

♦ ♦ ♦

The Lord lightens my darkness. II Samuel 22:29

♦ ♦ ♦

He is a shield unto all them that take refuge in Him.
II Samuel 22:31

♦ ♦ ♦

Fury is not in Me. Isaiah 27:4

♦ ♦ ♦

Let him take hold of My strength. Isaiah 27:5

♦ ♦ ♦

The Lord is a God of justice. Isaiah 30:18

◆ ◆ ◆

Have you not known…that the everlasting God, the Lord, the Creator of the ends of the earth, faints not, neither is weary? Isaiah 40:28

◆ ◆ ◆

The Lord shall be unto you an everlasting light, and your God your glory. Isaiah 60:19

◆ ◆ ◆

The Lord is good. Nahum 1:7

◆ ◆ ◆

I the Lord change not. Malachi 3:6

◆ ◆ ◆

The Lord is my strength and my shield. Psalm 28:7

◆ ◆ ◆

Oh how abundant is Your goodness. Psalm 31:20

◆ ◆ ◆

He loves righteousness and justice. Psalm 33:5

♦ ♦ ♦

The Lord loves justice. Psalm 37:28

♦ ♦ ♦

You are the God of my strength. Psalm 43:2

♦ ♦ ♦

Strength belongs to God. Psalm 62:12

♦ ♦ ♦

Surely the Lord's mercies are not consumed, surely His compassions fail not. They are new every morning. Lamentations 3:22-23

♦ ♦ ♦

He is the living God. Daniel 6:27

4

How I Can Come to Feel God's Love

Love isn't something we just pick out of the air—it stems from our innermost being.

In fact, Love is the very core of our being.

We can arrive logically at this conclusion.

What does each human being, each self, try to do? Each being tries to assert itself. What do we mean by self-assertion? We mean that each self-assertive being wants to be recognized, to be appreciated for itself. The desire for recognition and appreciation is just another way of saying each individual wants to be loved.

We next ask: What is Love? The answer is that Love is a dynamic process, a reciprocal process, a two-way process. Love is a Giving and Receiving.

To be loved, therefore, is to see in how many ways we receive. To love is to see in how many ways we give.

The two sides of Love are inseparable. Every action contains Giving and Receiving, Loving and Being Loved. Every being participates at every moment, in some form, in the Love Process of Life.

Significantly, therefore, the Love Force is fundamental to every being and every human being within Creation. There is no being so microscopic that it does not conform to this Universal Law and respond to this Universal Concept and operate according to this Universal Force.

Thus Love really does make the world go around, in the most profound and divine sense. The whole universe, which is a reflection and an expression of God, thus turns out to be a reflection and an expression of a God of Love.

We can say, therefore, that God is Love, God is a loving God, for He reflects and expresses only what He is.

How, then, can I come to feel God's Love?

First, by accepting the certainty, once and for all, that God, the universe, man, life are grounded in Love at all times, in all places, under all circumstances, for all eternity.

Second, by seeing how Love operates in your daily life in every event.

Third, by broadening your view to see Love at work everywhere around you, to the farthest corners of the universe.

Fourth, to look behind the appearances that seem to disprove the presence of Love. Reject these appearances, affirm the fundamental presence of Love, and find Love.

Fifth, practice Giving and Receiving, Loving and Being Loved. you are already doing it whether you intend to or not, because this is your nature. you are neither selfish nor unselfish, egoistic nor altruistic—you are both and you will always be both. Make yourself conscious of the two-fold Love in your life.

Sixth, live with the assurances of God's Love as expressed in many ways in the Bible. Let these assurances sink in, a phrase a day. The Bible is full of such expressions and assurances, in the Hebrew Bible (or "Old Testament"), and the New Testament.

Finally, remember that God's Love is expressed in other terms and ways. Justice is an aspect of Love. Law is an aspect of Love. Justice makes God fair. Law makes God dependable. A loving God must not only be a giving God, a compassionate God, a merciful God, He must also be a fair God and a dependable God.

<u>Verses</u>

The Lord is slow to anger and plenteous in loving-kindness. Numbers 14:18

◆　◆　◆

The Lord (forgives) iniquity and transgression. Numbers 14:18

◆　◆　◆

He will love you and bless you. Deuteronomy 7:13

♦ ♦ ♦

The Lord…has compassion upon His afflicted. Isaiah 49:13

♦ ♦ ♦

My kindness shall not depart from you…says the Lord that has compassion on you. Isaiah 54:10

♦ ♦ ♦

I am for you, and I will turn unto you. Ezekiel 36:9

♦ ♦ ♦

He is gracious and compassionate. Joel 2:13

♦ ♦ ♦

He is…long-suffering. Joel 2:13

♦ ♦ ♦

Remember, O Lord, Your compassions and Your mercies; for they have been from of old. Psalm 25:6

♦ ♦ ♦

I will be glad and rejoice in Your lovingkindness. Psalm 31:8

♦ ♦ ♦

Save me in Your lovingkindness. Psalm 31:17

♦ ♦ ♦

Blessed be the Lord; for He has shown me His wondrous lovingkindness. Psalm 31:22

♦ ♦ ♦

The earth is full of the lovingkindness of the Lord. Psalm 33:5

♦ ♦ ♦

How precious is Your lovingkindness, O God! Psalm 36:7

♦ ♦ ♦

Your lovingkindness is better than life. Psalm 63:4

♦ ♦ ♦

According to the multitude of Your compassions turn unto me. Psalm 69:17

♦ ♦ ♦

But You, O Lord, are a God full of compassion and graciousness, slow to anger, and plenteous in mercy and truth. Psalm 86:15

♦ ♦ ♦

When my cares are many within me, Your comforts delight my soul.
Psalm 94:19

♦ ♦ ♦

The Lord is gracious and full of compassion. Psalm 111:4

♦ ♦ ♦

Gracious is the Lord, and righteous; yes, our God is compassionate. Psalm 116:5

♦ ♦ ♦

The Lord is gracious and full of compassion; slow to anger, and of great mercy.
Psalm 145:8

♦ ♦ ♦

The Lord is good to all; and His tender mercies are over all His works.
Psalm 145:9

♦ ♦ ♦

The Lord…has compassion upon His afflicted. Isaiah 49:13

♦ ♦ ♦

I drew them…with bonds of love. Hosea 11:4

◆   ◆   ◆

He will be silent in His love. Zephaniah 3:17

5

How to Think of God's Ways

We tend to take God's measure in terms of man.

But God is far greater than we are. We keep losing sight of this because our sight remains focused upon earth. We look up in momentary surprise and wonder, once in a while, and see the stars.

We can, of course, see God's ways in terms of what happens to us here on earth. We ask, What does this mean? The answer which we receive tells us something about God's ways.

Our style of life, the emphasis of our life have been characterized by logic and reason. Our point of view has been critical and analytical. We have emphasized evidence, explanation, verification, facts, statistics, calculations and probabilities.

These aspects of the modern mind are present within God's mind as well, but we have become so impressed with our own prowess in this area that we have acted as if our thoughts must inevitably be God's thoughts, our conclusions must be God's conclusions, our vision must be God's vision, our expectations must be God's expectations, our judgments must be God's judgments, our plans must be God's plans, our ways must be God's ways.

We have gone overboard in this direction. We must learn to separate ourselves from our exaggerated self-confidence; we must start looking beyond our confined mentalities; we must try to become aware of the fact that our knowledge of God's ways is but a speck compared with what we do not know of God's ways.

We must develop this kind of attitude so that we can live with a greater faith from day to day, when the details of our lives seem to confuse us in our effort to make sense out of them.

It is only in retrospect that we see over and over again how events that we did not understand or that we complained about really proved to be part of a larger pattern that assumed meaning in time.

It is often in retrospect that we realize that the benefits of what actually happened as opposed to what we had wished for proved far greater.

At such time we usually promise ourselves to remember this lesson in the future, only to again forget.

The way to maintain this kind of attitude consistently is by a shift in emphasis. We must start relying more on God's mind than on our mind; we must learn to trust more in God's logic than our logic; we must begin freeing ourselves from trying to call all the shots and develop a confidence in God's ways.

We must recognize our limitations. We must work within our limitations. We must do all we can and then, beyond this, turn all things, including ourselves, over to God.

<u>Verses</u>

And God saw every thing that He had made, and, behold, it was very good. Genesis 1:31

◆ ◆ ◆

He will not fail you, neither destroy you. Deuteronomy 4:31

◆ ◆ ◆

The secret things belong unto the Lord our God; but the things that are revealed belong unto us and to our children forever. Deuteronomy 29:14

◆ ◆ ◆

My thoughts are not your thoughts, neither are your ways My ways, says the Lord. Isaiah 55:8

◆ ◆ ◆

For as the heavens are higher than the earth, so are My ways higher than your ways, and My thoughts than your thoughts. Isaiah 55:9

I the Lord love justice. Isaiah 61:8

♦ ♦ ♦

I am with you to save you and to deliver you, says the Lord. Jeremiah 15:20

♦ ♦ ♦

I am God, and not man. Hosea 12:9

♦ ♦ ♦

As for God, His way is perfect. Psalm 18:31

♦ ♦ ♦

The word of the Lord is tried. Psalm 18:31

♦ ♦ ♦

O consider and see that the Lord is good. Psalm 34:9

♦ ♦ ♦

The Lord is righteous in all His ways, and gracious in all His works. Psalm 145:17

◆   ◆   ◆

Have You eyes of flesh, or do You see as man sees? Job 10:4

◆   ◆   ◆

Can you find out the deep things of God? Job 11:7

◆   ◆   ◆

Yes, of a surety, God will not do wickedly, neither will the Almighty pervert justice. Job 34:12

◆   ◆   ◆

Great is Your faithfulness. Lamentations 3:23

6

How I Can Always Be Sure of Mercy from God

The universe operates according to laws. Our lives are governed by these spiritual laws. If we observe these laws we feel free and our life runs smoothly; if we violate these laws we are enslaved and our life becomes a mess.

It could be said that we are rewarded or punished depending on whether we observe or violate these laws.

If there were no laws, there would be no order in the universe and life would be totally chaotic and undependable.

Since God is a just God, His laws are just. Since God is a fair God, he treats everyone alike. We are all ruled by the same laws. This is God's justice.

God's love requires that He be a just God. But it also requires that He be a merciful God.

God's justice can hurt. We make mistakes, knowingly or unknowingly, and we suffer the consequences. Sometimes these consequences can be full of anguish, shame, and terror.

It is when life is unbearable, especially as a result of some deed we have done, that we wonder whether God still wants to have anything to do with us. When nobody else wants us, why would God?

The remarkable thing is that God never deserts us—He is always part of us and we are always part of Him. We are inseparable, even when we turn our back on Him and deny Him.

What is God's attitude then in time of crisis?

He will not change His laws for us. We must accept the consequences of our actions, painful as this might be. But he will be with us. When everyone else has deserted us, when everyone else has turned his back on us, when everyone else has turned against us, God will be with us in mercy and in love.

He will not love us for any wrong deed, but He will love us because He knows that we need His love.

His mercy consists in this—that even the worst and the most heinous deed can be and will be transformed to serve God, regardless of our intentions to the contrary.

This is why God can offer us mercy personally, if we so desire.

If we desire to turn night into day, mourning into joy, death into life, this is the mercy that He offers us personally—that we place our life at His service and that we see how we can serve Him, wherever we stand and wherever God might lead us.

What must we do? We must turn to Him in submission and contrition.

<u>Verses</u>

The Lord your God is a merciful God. Deuteronomy 4:31

◆ ◆ ◆

Let us fall now into the hand of the Lord; for His mercies are great; and let me not fall into the hand of man. II Samuel 24:14

◆ ◆ ◆

I have blotted out…your transgressions, and…your sins. Isaiah 44:22

◆ ◆ ◆

Have I any pleasure at all that the wicked should die? says the Lord God; and not rather that he should return from his ways, and live? Ezekiel 18:23

◆ ◆ ◆

He is…abundant in mercy. Joel 2:13

♦ ♦ ♦

But as for me, in Your mercy do I trust. Psalm 13:6

♦ ♦ ♦

According to Your mercy remember me. Psalm 25:7

♦ ♦ ♦

Your mercy is before my eyes; and I have walked in Your truth. Psalm 26:3

♦ ♦ ♦

I acknowledged my sin to You…and You, You forgave the iniquity of my sin. Psalm 32:5

♦ ♦ ♦

Let Your mercy and Your truth continually preserve me. Psalm 40:12

♦ ♦ ♦

The mercy of God endures continually. Psalm 52:3

♦ ♦ ♦

Be gracious unto me, O God, be gracious unto me. Psalm 57:2

◆ ◆ ◆

You, O Lord, are good, and ready to pardon, and plenteous in mercy unto all them that call upon you. Psalm 86:5

◆ ◆ ◆

Great is Your mercy toward me. Psalm 86:13

◆ ◆ ◆

If I say: "My foot slips," Your mercy, O Lord, holds me up. Psalm 94:18

◆ ◆ ◆

The Lord is good; His mercy endures forever. Psalm 100:5

◆ ◆ ◆

I will sing of mercy and justice. Psalm 101:1

◆ ◆ ◆

Let Your tender mercies come unto me, that I may live. Psalm 119:77

7

How to Make All Things Work for You

One of the greatest gifts that God has built into life is the Law of Transformation.

By this law, life overcomes death.

By this law, good triumphs over evil.

By this law, mercy enters justice.

Every moment of our being, every event of our life can be used for the sake of life and can be transformed to serve God.

This is the salvation at the heart of all being.

Life challenges us in many ways. We work towards success and it is delayed. We desire love and we cannot find the right partner. We are handicapped financially, physically, socially, geographically. The time and the place are against us. We are too young, we are too old. We are in the wrong field. We face personal tragedies and disappointments. Things happen which we cannot undo.

There is only one thing that we can do. There is only one thing that we must do. There is only one thing that we need do: we must transform the event.

We must give a creative answer to life; we must give an affirmative answer to life; we must transform life to serve life.

This is how we can win when we have lost; this is how we can succeed when we have failed; this is how we can go on living when we feel we cannot go on living; this is how we can find new life when we look back in dismay at the old life; this is how we are born again—in this life, and in the life to come.

There are no dead ends. Every event can be transformed. Every event can be seen as a gift from God and a gift to God. It is more important THAT we serve, than HOW we serve.

This attitude is also the key to the puzzling problem of Good and Evil.

It is obvious and undeniable that there is evil in the world. Men commit terrible deeds. We must remember, first of all, that these deeds are committed by men, not God.

We blame God for the presence of evil; we must blame man. Evil occurs because God has given us freedom of choice. If He had not, we would be robots. But we are created in the image of God, who is free to choose at every moment of being. We, being a part of God, are also free to choose at every moment of our being. As we misinterpret the nature of life, as we rebel against the laws of life, we make choices that introduce evil into the world.

God does not prevent us form making a wrong choice but does not grant evil the error of its ways or the victory of its direction.

God turns evil against itself, so that it achieves the opposite of its intentions. Evil produces revulsion, opposition, division, distrust, hate and disgust. Evil produces an opposite thrust to the degree and to the extent of its presence.

Thus does God make evil serve the forces of good that are basic to the universe. God transforms evil, so that it serves instead of rules.

We can turn all things to the service of life. We can transform life, which is constantly transformed. We must accept all the consequences of our deeds. As we find a way to serve, we enter into God's presence and protection and we discover His mercy in this life and in the life to come.

<u>Verses</u>

Him shall you serve. Deuteronomy 10:20

◆ ◆ ◆

The Lord your God turned the curse into a blessing unto you, because the Lord your God loves you. Deuteronomy 23:6

◆ ◆ ◆

I will make all My mountains a way. Isaiah 49:11

◆ ◆ ◆

You shall forget the shame of your youth. Isaiah 54:4

◆ ◆ ◆

Incline your ear, and come unto Me. Hear, and your soul shall live. Isaiah 55:3

◆ ◆ ◆

Let him return unto the Lord, and He will have compassion upon him, and to our God, for He will abundantly pardon. Isaiah 55:7

◆ ◆ ◆

If the wicked turn from all his sins…and do that which is lawful and right, he shall surely live, he shall not die. Ezekiel 18:21

◆ ◆ ◆

The Lord my God does lighten my darkness. Psalm 18:29

◆ ◆ ◆

You did turn my mourning into dancing. Psalm 30:12

◆ ◆ ◆

Bring my soul out of prison. Psalm 142:8

◆　◆　◆

The Lord is good to all; and his tender mercies are over all His works.
Psalm 145:9

◆　◆　◆

The righteous, even when he is brought to death, has hope. Proverbs 14:32

◆　◆　◆

Victory is of the Lord. Proverbs 21:31

◆　◆　◆

What? Shall we receive good at the hand of God, and shall we not receive evil?
Job 2:10

◆　◆　◆

(But) the way of the wicked he makes crooked. Psalm 146:9

8

How to Overcome Fear

I am subject to many fears as a human being.
   I can fear for my life.
   I can fear for my job.
   I can fear for my future.
   I can fear for the future of my family.
   The day can be full of fears.
   I may fear various individuals that I must deal with.
   I may live in frightening surroundings and in fearful times.
   I may have money fears.
   I may fear failure.
   I may fear losing what I have or not gaining what I desire.
   I need relief from all my fears. I need protection against my fears. I need a way of triumphing over my fears.
   Drinking won't do it. Smoking won't do it. Eating won't do it. The pursuit of pleasure, power or wealth won't do it. These are coverups that don't cover up.
   But God does offer relief from my fears. God does provide protection against my fears. God does help me to triumph over my fears.
   I affirm that God is with me at all times and under all circumstances. I am never alone.
   I think of myself as being directly responsible to God and no one else. In case of conflict, my responsibility is to God, not men.
   I affirm that God provides for all my needs, that He knows my needs, that He works through many channels to satisfy my needs, and that I must develop confidence in His workings and in the instruments through which He works.
   I know that just as God is with me, so is He with every being of His creation, including those I love. I can count on Him to help them as He helps me. I can also count on His presence in every being, even when this does not seem apparent. I can trust in a Presence and Power greater than mine.

I can bear all things better knowing that God recognizes my effort, and appreciates my effort, and rewards my effort. I can bear all things better knowing that there is Someone Else who knows what I am going through, and who helps me bear my situation. I can bear all things better knowing that doing so is serving God in a special way, even though it may be hard to do and hard to understand. I can bear all things better knowing that I will always be a part of God. I can bear all things better knowing that God's spirit, of which I am a part, is indestructible. I can bear all things better knowing that God expresses His love to me, and that I can express my love for Him, in every encounter with life, including every moment of suffering.

I can rise above fear by lifting my spirit to God. I can rise above fear through union with God.

<u>Verses</u>

Fear not, for I am with you, and will bless you. Genesis 26:24

♦ ♦ ♦

Fear not, stand still, and see the salvation of the Lord, which he will work for you today. Exodus 14:13

♦ ♦ ♦

You shall not be afraid of the face of any man. Deuteronomy 1:17

♦ ♦ ♦

Fear not. Deuteronomy 31:6

♦ ♦ ♦

Be not dismayed, for I am your God. Isaiah 41:10

◆ ◆ ◆

Who are you, that you are afraid of man that shall die? Isaiah 51:12

◆ ◆ ◆

You shall not fear evil any more. Zephaniah 3:15

◆ ◆ ◆

The Lord is my light and my salvation: whom shall I fear? Psalm 27:1

◆ ◆ ◆

The Lord is the stronghold of my life; of whom shall I be afraid? Psalm 27:1

◆ ◆ ◆

Though war should rise up against me, even then will I be confident. Psalm 27:3

◆ ◆ ◆

We (will) not fear, though the earth do change. Psalm 46:3

◆ ◆ ◆

In the day when I am afraid, I will put my trust in You. Psalm 56:4

9

How to See Myself

We talk about people having a good or bad self-image.

Is there a justification for a good self-image? How can we get rid of a bad self-image?

The key to this matter is the fact that we are created in God's image. We are expressions of God. God has implanted His spirit within us.

This does not mean that we are God, but it means that we share in His qualities, His nature, His being. To the extent that we reflect these qualities, we are God-like. We can remain God-like or become God-like by working on these qualities.

God is merciful, abundant, just, generous, loving, kind, vital, creative, unafraid, strong, good, friendly.

I am all of these, actually or potentially.

I am created in His image. By dwelling on His image, I can bring out the best within myself.

Verses

And God created man in His own image, in the image of God created He him. Genesis 1:27

◆ ◆ ◆

I have set the Lord always before me. Psalm 16:8

◆   ◆   ◆

I shall be satisfied, when I awake, with Thy likeness. Psalm 17:15

10

How I Don't Have to Worry about What Others Think, Say, or Do

We get all hung up because of the opinions of others.

We are especially affected by family relationships—mother, father, brother, sister, husband, wife, in-laws, children.

We get caught up in their patterns of dealing with us. They can manipulate us. They can make us do things we don't want to do. They can make us feel good or bad with a word, a look, a tone of voice.

We feel trapped, victimized. We let it happen again and again out of fear of what happens when we say "no" and out of a desire to win approval.

We are anxious to please, but the truth is we can never please enough nor can we ever please once and for all.

This is tyranny—being at the mercy of the whims of other human beings.

This is idolatry—idolizing and worshiping another human being by looking to him or her for ultimate approval and authority.

This is slavery—placing ourselves in bondage to another mortal.

We do this in many ways, not only in family relationships. We do this with friends, with fellow workers, with employers, with business contacts.

People get to us. They know what buttons to push to make us jump.

Naturally, we want to be sensitive to people and we want to be a part of them. But we don't want to deal with others at the expense of our dignity. We desire respect for our rights and understanding for our position.

This whole problem changes when we permit God to enter the picture.

The reason is simple.

The minute we make God our ultimate concern we replace some human being to whom, consciously or unconsciously, we have given this power heretofore.

The minute we look to God for understanding, we no longer need to appeal so desperately for such understanding from some human being whom we have cast in this role.

The minute we look to God for approval, we no longer need turn flip-flops for some human being whose continuous approval we court but fail to achieve.

God is much easier to please than any human being.

God is much more understanding and generous.

God frees us from our enslavements.

God actually makes it possible to deal better with our fellow human beings, including the closest members of the family.

By addressing ourselves to God, we can close our ears to those unpleasant sounds of human beings that before dried up our desire to help.

By trying to please God, we can stop trying to please everybody.

By acknowledging God, we can stop making gods out of human beings.

By making God supreme, we can stop giving other beings ultimate authority over our spirit.

<u>Verses</u>

The Lord shall reign for ever and ever. Exodus 15:18

◆ ◆ ◆

All the earth is mine. Exodus 19:5

◆ ◆ ◆

You shall have no other gods before me. Exodus 20:3

◆ ◆ ◆

You shall bow down to no other god. Exodus 34:14

♦ ♦ ♦

Rebel not against the Lord, neither fear the people of the land. Numbers 14:9

♦ ♦ ♦

Unto you it was shown, that you might know that the Lord, He is God. Deuteronomy 4:35

♦ ♦ ♦

Know this day, and lay it to heart, that the Lord, He is God in heaven above and upon the earth beneath; there is none else. Deuteronomy 4:39

♦ ♦ ♦

Beware lest you forget the Lord your God…and you say in your heart: "My power and the might of my hand have gotten me this wealth." Deuteronomy 8:11-17

♦ ♦ ♦

There is none beside You. I Samuel 2:2

♦ ♦ ♦

You are the God, even you alone, of all the kingdoms of the earth. II Kings 19:15

♦ ♦ ♦

I, even I, am the Lord; and beside Me there is no savior. Isaiah 43:11

Your God reigns! Isaiah 52:7

◆ ◆ ◆

There is nothing too hard for You. Jeremiah 32:17

◆ ◆ ◆

For the kingdom is the Lord's. Psalm 22:29

◆ ◆ ◆

The earth is the Lord's. Psalm 23:24

◆ ◆ ◆

Put not your trust in princes, nor in the son of man, in whom there is no help. Psalm 146:3

◆ ◆ ◆

The fear of man brings a snare; but whoso puts his trust in the Lord shall be set up on high. Proverbs 29:25

◆ ◆ ◆

Declare, if you know it all. Job 38:18

◆   ◆   ◆

Yours, O Lord, is the greatness, and the power, and the glory, and the victory, and the majesty. I Chronicles 29:11

11

How I Can Become Confident of God's Personal Concern for Me

Many individuals have a vague concept of God. God is a Force, God is a Principle, God is an Abstraction to them.

They think of God in an impersonal way. They feel that even if He has being, He is far too great to really be directly aware of individual human beings.

They think that it is foolish to believe that each one of us is known to God.

It is not foolish at all. In fact, it is quite reasonable to believe that God knows each one of us.

Let us look at the matter from two directions.

To begin with, an impersonal God does not interest me. I can't pray to a Process. I can't talk to a Principle. I can't love a Force. I can't find comfort from some Inner Law or Remote Being. I couldn't care about an Absentee Lord who cares for me in general, but who couldn't care about me in particular.

I need love, understanding, assurance, certainty, at all times. No one on earth can give me this. God alone can give me this. I need a personal God who loves me, understands me, reassures me, and gives me a sense of certainty at every moment of my being.

Am I asking too much? No.

At first glance it may seem so. It may even appear foolish to think that someone like God is directly aware of me and my seemingly trivial concerns.

But it's neither foolish nor illogical.

When we think of God, we generally think of His grandeur, which we visualize in terms of a universe so vast that it staggers the imagination. We view God's grandeur through the telescope, and we forget to view it through the microscope. The world in miniature is as staggering to the imagination as the world of the planets and the stars and the solar systems. That God created the ant is as fantastic as that He created the Milky Way.

If God has no trouble thinking big, He has no trouble thinking small. If He can create a universe, He can install an intercom system that connects Him directly to every being and every human being within Creation.

If man can create a walkie-talkie, God can. If man can invent a transistor radio, God can.

We are wired for direct communion with God. He is a grand, a marvelous Personal God.

<u>Verses</u>

Come near before the Lord. Exodus 16:9

◆ ◆ ◆

I know you by name. Exodus 33:17

◆ ◆ ◆

He has known your walking through this great wilderness. Deuteronomy 2:7

◆ ◆ ◆

I poured out my soul before the Lord. I Samuel 1:15

◆ ◆ ◆

With my soul have I desired You in the night. Isaiah 26:9

◆ ◆ ◆

"I have called you by your name, you are Mine." Isaiah 43:1

◆ ◆ ◆

"You are precious in My sight and honorable, and I have loved you." Isaiah 43:4

◆ ◆ ◆

Surely God is in you. Isaiah 45:14

◆ ◆ ◆

"I am with you," says the Lord. Haggai 1:13

◆ ◆ ◆

"I have chosen you," says the Lord. Haggai 2:23

◆ ◆ ◆

I call unto the Lord, and he answers me. Psalm 3:5

◆ ◆ ◆

The Lord will hear when I call unto Him. Psalm 4:4

◆ ◆ ◆

The Lord receives my prayer. Psalm 6:10

◆ ◆ ◆

Examine me, O Lord, and try me; test my reins and my heart.
Psalm 26:2

◆ ◆ ◆

Lord, be you my helper. Psalm 30:11

◆ ◆ ◆

Behold, God is my helper. Psalm 54:6

◆ ◆ ◆

He has delivered me out of all trouble. Psalm 54:9

◆ ◆ ◆

This I know, that God is for me. Psalm 56:10

◆ ◆ ◆

You have delivered my soul from death. Psalm 56:14

◆ ◆ ◆

O God, You are my God. Psalm 63:2

♦ ♦ ♦

My soul thirsts for You, my flesh longs for You, in a dry and weary land, where no water is. Psalm 63:2

♦ ♦ ♦

But as for me, the nearness of God is my good. Psalm 73:28

♦ ♦ ♦

He that planted the ear, shall He not hear? Psalm 94:9

♦ ♦ ♦

He that formed the eye, shall He not see? Psalm 94:9

♦ ♦ ♦

The Lord knows the thoughts of man. Psalm 94:11

♦ ♦ ♦

The Lord is for me; I will not fear; what can man do unto me? Psalm 118:6

♦ ♦ ♦

The Lord is my strength and song; and He is become my salvation. Psalm 118:14

◆ ◆ ◆

The Lord is your keeper. Psalm 121:5

◆ ◆ ◆

You know Your servant. I Chronicles 17:18

◆ ◆ ◆

Is not the Lord your God with you? I Chronicles 22:18

◆ ◆ ◆

The Lord God, even my God, is with you. I Chronicles 28:20

12

God as Helper, or, How to Relax

We are uptight about life. We are tense, nervous, worried. We are under constant pressure.

We worry about everything: getting a job, holding a job, finding a better job; getting through school, getting to college, staying in college; finding the right marriage partner, getting married, supporting a wife and family, paying the bills, paying for the children's present and future education, providing for the retirement years.

Every day is full of worries about ourselves and about the world.

There is no question but that life is a constant problem-solving activity from moment to moment. There are matters that require our immediate attention and there are matters that require our eventual attention.

These things don't get done by themselves. We must tackle them and we are expected to do our share of the work. Otherwise, nothing happens or the wrong thing happens.

But most of us go too far. It's right to feel that we must pull our own weight and do our share. But most of us are really trying to do more than our share. Most of us are trying to pull the weight of the universe—our way.

Most of us feel we must call all the shots. We refuse to let George—or God—do anything. We don't trust either one of them.

But George does do a lot and God does even more, lots more. What's more, they are quite trustworthy.

Much of our uptight trouble stems from the fact that we try to control, force, and manipulate life. We not only think we have to do this, we think we can do this. We have the mistaken notion that it's all up to us. It isn't.

We are limited in what we can do.

We are limited in intelligence, vision, power, and life itself. We are limited by individuals and circumstances over which we have no control and which we can neither predict nor anticipate. We are limited by the finiteness and mortality of our being.

To act otherwise is to act in a distorted manner and to bring about the distorted attitudes and feelings that create an unbearable uptight condition.

Only God has total control. Only God has full vision. Only God has infinite power. Only God really knows what's best for all concerned. Only God has unlimited intelligence. Only God knows all the factors of a situation.

We must recognize the fact that God is very much concerned with His Creation, including every being within Creation. We have to do our share, but God never asked us to go it alone. God is with us constantly, working out details that we are not even aware of, setting forces in motion that we cannot even see, considering factors that we do not even grasp.

We are not here alone, and we don't have to go it alone. We cannot do it alone, and we are not asked to do it alone.

God is working through many channels for our good and the good of each individual being at all times. We must open our eyes to see in how many ways help comes to us constantly. We must start to see this as God working with us and for us. We must not despair when things do not go our way or there is an annoying delay. We must make even such situations serve our purposes. Often we see their greater value and deeper wisdom in retrospect.

God is never absent from our side. Among His qualities, God is also a Helper. We must think of Him and call on Him in this capacity and, as we do so, we not only begin to relax, but we go on to even greater joy and achievement.

<u>Verses</u>

Is any thing too hard for the Lord? Genesis 18:14

◆ ◆ ◆

The Lord your God, He it is that fights for you. Deuteronomy 3:22

◆ ◆ ◆

He drew me out of many waters. II Samuel 22:17

By my God do I scale a wall. II Samuel 22:30

◆ ◆ ◆

He gives power to the faint. Isaiah 40:29

◆ ◆ ◆

To him that has no might, He increases strength. Isaiah 40:29

◆ ◆ ◆

They that wait for the Lord shall renew their strength. Isaiah 40:31

◆ ◆ ◆

They that wait for the Lord…shall run, and not be weary. Isaiah 40:31

◆ ◆ ◆

I strengthen you, yes, I help you. Isaiah 41:10

◆ ◆ ◆

I uphold you with my victorious right hand. Isaiah 41:10

◆ ◆ ◆

I help you, says the Lord, and your Redeemer, the Holy One. Isaiah 41:14

◆ ◆ ◆

I, the Lord…have taken hold of your hand. Isaiah 42:6

◆ ◆ ◆

I will go before you, and make the crooked places straight. Isaiah 45:2

◆ ◆ ◆

Look unto Me, and be saved, all the ends of the earth; for I am God and there is none else. Isaiah 45:22

◆ ◆ ◆

Look unto me and be saved. Isaiah 45:22

◆ ◆ ◆

I am the Lord your God, who teaches you for your profit. Isaiah 48:17

◆ ◆ ◆

Have I no power to deliver? Isaiah 50:2

◆ ◆ ◆

The Lord God will help me. Isaiah 50:7

◆ ◆ ◆

You shall know that I the Lord am your savior. Isaiah 60:16

◆ ◆ ◆

Turn you to your God. Hosea 12:7

◆ ◆ ◆

Beside Me there is no savior. Hosea 13:4

◆ ◆ ◆

Whosoever shall call on the name of the Lord shall be delivered. Joel 3:5

◆ ◆ ◆

Wait for me, says the Lord. Zephaniah 3:8

◆ ◆ ◆

You eat, but you have not enough. Haggai 1:6

◆ ◆ ◆

You drink, but you are not filled with drink. Haggai 1:6

◆ ◆ ◆

You clothe yourself, but there is none warm. Haggai 1:6

◆ ◆ ◆

You deliver me from the violent man. Psalm 18:49

◆ ◆ ◆

He will bring forth my feet out of the net. Psalm 25:15

◆ ◆ ◆

You have been my help. Psalm 27:9

◆ ◆ ◆

For though my father and my mother have forsaken me, the Lord will take me up. Psalm 27:10

◆ ◆ ◆

Lead me in an even path. Psalm 27:11

♦ ♦ ♦

The Lord is near unto them that are of a broken heart, and saves such as are of a contrite spirit. Psalm 34:19

♦ ♦ ♦

Many are the ills of the righteous, but the Lord delivers him out of them all. Psalm 34:20

♦ ♦ ♦

The Lord helps…he delivers…from the wicked, and saves. Psalms 37:40

♦ ♦ ♦

You are my help and my deliverer. Psalm 40:18

♦ ♦ ♦

For God, he is judge. Psalm 50:6

♦ ♦ ♦

Our God comes, and does not keep silence. Psalm 50:3

♦ ♦ ♦

Cast your burden upon the Lord, and He will sustain you. Psalm 55:23

◆ ◆ ◆

God is unto us a God of deliverances. Psalm 68:21

◆ ◆ ◆

Give Your strength unto Your servant. Psalm 86:16

◆ ◆ ◆

The Lord is for me as my helper. Psalm 118:7

◆ ◆ ◆

It is better to take refuge in the Lord than to trust in princes. Psalm 118:9

◆ ◆ ◆

Cause me to know the way wherein I should walk. Psalm 143:8

◆ ◆ ◆

He is a shield to them that walk in integrity. Proverbs 2:7

◆ ◆ ◆

He delivers and rescues. Daniel 6:27

13

How to Be Happy

We want to be happy.

We have different ways of putting it, but essentially we would like to be happy—all the time.

We are meant to be happy.

God wants us to be happy.

We may have to learn the best ways of being happy, but happiness, here and now, is within reach and is meant to be achieved.

We must remind ourselves of this as often as possible.

We are told this frequently in the Bible itself.

We are also told what leads to happiness.

We can be happy even while learning to be happy.

We can achieve a spiritual happiness under all circumstances and conditions.

Happiness is finding God.

Happiness is serving God.

Happiness is knowing that God loves me.

Happiness is being important to God.

Happiness is giving life meaning through God.

Happiness is being aware at all times of God's presence.

Happiness is having a personal God.

Happiness is knowing that God is personally concerned about me.

Happiness is having God as helper.

Happiness is learning to understand and live by God's dependable laws.

Happiness is finding built-in rewards constantly according to the Law of Giving and Receiving.

Happiness is knowing that God is just and merciful.

Happiness is never being without God.

Happiness is being created in God's image.

Verses

To love the Lord your God, to hearken to His voice, and to cleave unto Him; for that is your life, and the length of your days. Deuteronomy 30:20

◆ ◆ ◆

Happy are all they that wait for Him. Isaiah 30:18

◆ ◆ ◆

There is hope for your future, says the Lord. Jeremiah 31:16

◆ ◆ ◆

Serve the Lord. Psalm 2:11

◆ ◆ ◆

Happy are all they that take refuge in Him. Psalm 2:12

◆ ◆ ◆

Happy is the man that takes refuge in Him. Psalm 34:9

◆ ◆ ◆

Happy the man that has made the Lord his trust. Psalm 40:5

◆ ◆ ◆

Happy are they that dwell in Your house. Psalm 84:5

◆ ◆ ◆

Happy is the man that finds wisdom. Proverbs 3:13

14

How to Become Trusting

Life is trustworthy in many ways.

It is dependable. It operates according to universal laws that I can learn and put to use.

Life has meaning. Every being serves God in some special way.

Life is indestructible. Every being is a revelation of God's Spirit which manifests itself in many forms but which is indestructible.

Life continues. We can transform everything that happens to serve the cause of life. There are no dead ends. Every end is also a new beginning.

Life is Loving and Being Loved, life is Giving and Receiving. This truth is present in every situation. It means that we are rewarded continuously and instantly. It also means that we are giving generously to life in some way at all times.

Life is lofty. We are created in God's image. We are part of God. We participate in God and in His ongoing Creation. We are necessary to God, because he does not create any being needlessly. Our task is to serve God in whatever way we find. We are never without God.

Life isn't all up to us. We have to do our share. We have to figure things out as best we can. But there is a Power greater than we are, namely, God, who takes care of matters beyond our control. As we are concerned about life, we can be assured that He is even more concerned.

Life is underwritten by God. This is our guarantee that life has meaning and purpose, and that we have a personal stake in it.

Life presents us with a personal God. We are always with God, and He communicates with us and knows us personally.

These are some of the worthwhile qualities that can be found in life. There are many others. They can all be tested repeatedly. They stand up to analysis and experimentation.

They can be trusted.

As we remind ourselves frequently of these aspects, and as we see evidence of them in our own lives, we develop confidence and trust in their reliability.

This trust and this confidence help shape our attitudes and actions, for the better.

<u>Verses</u>

Am I in the place of God? Genesis 50:19

◆ ◆ ◆

The Lord will fight for you, and you shall hold your peace. Exodus 14:14

◆ ◆ ◆

Be of good courage. Numbers 13:20

◆ ◆ ◆

You shall not try the Lord your God. Deuteronomy 6:16

◆ ◆ ◆

Be strong and of good courage. Deuteronomy 31:6

◆ ◆ ◆

Behold, God is my salvation; I will trust and not be afraid. Isaiah 12:2

◆ ◆ ◆

Blessed is the man that trusts in the Lord. Jeremiah 17:7

◆　◆　◆

Wait for your God continually. Hosea 12:7

◆　◆　◆

Put your trust in the Lord. Psalm 4:6

◆　◆　◆

For You do I wait all the day. Psalm 25:5

◆　◆　◆

Wait for the Lord. Psalm 27:14

◆　◆　◆

Be strong, and let your heart take courage; yes, wait for the Lord. Psalm 27:14

◆　◆　◆

In Him has my heart trusted, and I am helped.
Psalm 26:7

◆　◆　◆

He that trusts in the Lord, mercy compasses him about. Psalm 32:10

♦ ♦ ♦

Trust also in Him, and He will bring it to pass. Psalm 37:5

♦ ♦ ♦

Resign yourself unto the Lord, and wait patiently for Him. Psalm 37:7

♦ ♦ ♦

I trust in the mercy of God for ever and ever. Psalm 52:11

♦ ♦ ♦

In God do I trust, I will not be afraid; what can man do unto me? Psalm 56:12

♦ ♦ ♦

But as for me, I know that my Redeemer lives. Job 19:25

15

How to Find Meaning in My Life

We want our life to have purpose. We want it to have meaning.

We look to some people enviously and say, "Oh, he's doing something important."

Most of us really consider our work unimportant. We consider our lives humdrum and routine. If only we could be important. If only we could do something important.

We try different ways of giving importance to our existence.

If we don't find real satisfaction in our work, we find a cause to work for. We find a hobby to pursue that gives us satisfaction. We join organizations.

But sooner or later the original glow wears off. Sooner or later the flaws start to show. Sooner or later the goal, rather than being realized, disappears farther and farther into some distant future, if it does not vanish from sight altogether.

We become disillusioned with individuals whom we once saw in ideal terms. We become disenchanted with causes as we see the disappointing inner workings of organizations. We lose faith in goals as they prove harder of achievement than we ever expected.

We go from hope to despair, from optimism to pessimism, from belief to cynicism, from meaning to absurdity, from abundant living to inner bankruptcy.

The pattern repeats itself as we change loyalties from person to person, group to group, cause to cause.

God alone offers the way out. It's the best way. It's the perfect way. It's a way that works.

God created me. God called me into life. God chose me. I am an instrument of God. God expresses Himself through me. God acts through me.

This is a fantastic concept, once it sinks in. It means that there is a direct connection between me and God. It means there is a direct relationship between me and God. It means that I have value to God right here and now, in place and time.

The great truth of my existence is that I am here to serve God. There are no great or small deeds, there are no important or unimportant works. How great, really, is the greatest human deed, how important, really, is the most important human work, relative to the immeasurable size of the universe and the greatness of God?

God alone is the guarantee for our life. With His backing, life is meaningful; without His backing, life is absurd.

I am important to God. As I take on importance, everything I do assumes importance.

By placing myself at God's service, everything I do takes on meaning. I dedicate everything I do to God—my daily work, my every thought. All the trivial things of daily living, all the dull duties of ordinary existence now take on a new look. I can see them as ways in which I serve God. I realize that there are not just one or two ways of serving Him, but that the ways are endless in their colorful variety. I realize that serving God is not reserved to the few, but generously granted to all beings.

I find that as I do things for the sake of God, I can serve creatively as long as I live. My energy comes from God. It does not dry up because of the flaws of human beings and human institutions. My reward also comes from God—life, instead of death.

God, unlike man, is constant.

<u>Verses</u>

Be a blessing. Genesis 12:2

◆　　◆　　◆

In you shall all the families of the earth be blessed. Genesis 12:3

◆　　◆　　◆

Consecrate yourselves today to the Lord. Exodus 32:29

◆ ◆ ◆

You shall be holy, for I am holy. Leviticus 11:45

◆ ◆ ◆

What does the Lord your God require of you, but…to serve the Lord your God with all your heart and with all your soul. Deuteronomy 10:12

◆ ◆ ◆

To Him shall you cleave. Deuteronomy 10:20

◆ ◆ ◆

I will proclaim the name of the Lord. Deuteronomy 32:3

◆ ◆ ◆

Serve the Lord. Joshua 24:14

◆ ◆ ◆

And if it seem evil unto you to serve the Lord, choose you this day whom you will serve. Joshua 24:15

◆ ◆ ◆

Incline your heart unto the Lord. Joshua 24:23

♦ ♦ ♦

How long do you halt between two opinions? If the Lord be God, follow Him; but if Baal, follow him. I Kings 18:21

♦ ♦ ♦

Turn unto Him against whom you have deeply rebelled. Isaiah 31:6

♦ ♦ ♦

You are my servant. Isaiah 41:9

♦ ♦ ♦

I have chosen you and not cast you away. Isaiah 41:9

♦ ♦ ♦

I have formed you, you are my own servant. Isaiah 44:21

♦ ♦ ♦

All souls are Mine. Ezekiel 18:4

♦ ♦ ♦

Consider your ways. Haggai 1:6

◆ ◆ ◆

But as for me, in the abundance of Your lovingkindness will I come into Your house. Psalm 5:8

◆ ◆ ◆

I will tell of all Your marvelous works. Psalm 9:2

◆ ◆ ◆

Declare among the peoples His doings. Psalm 9:12

◆ ◆ ◆

Let the words of my mouth and the meditation of my heart be acceptable before You, O Lord, my Rock, and my Redeemer. Psalm 19:15

◆ ◆ ◆

Unto You, O Lord, do I lift my soul. Psalm 25:1

◆ ◆ ◆

My eyes are ever toward the Lord. Psalm 25:15

◆ ◆ ◆

Worship the Lord in the beauty of holiness. Psalm 29:2

♦ ♦ ♦

All nations shall serve Him. Psalm 72:11

♦ ♦ ♦

Beside You I desire none upon earth. Psalm 73:25

♦ ♦ ♦

Many seek the ruler's favor: but a man's judgment comes from the Lord. Proverbs 29:26

♦ ♦ ♦

Though he slay me, yet will I trust Him. Job 13:15

16

How to Develop a Right Attitude

We must accept the reality of life as it is.

We are not going to change God. He is what He is. So is His Creation, being an expression of God.

For maximum results, we must accept the established system of life and work in terms of it.

The universe is governed by certain rules and regulations. We must work with these rules and regulations.

This is often hard to do. We seem to be born against our will, and we seem to die against our will. In between, things happen which we don't like. We are angry at life, and we don't really care for the system. We really want to rebel against it, and we do in many ways.

What we should do really is to make the best of it. We say we do, but we really don't.

To make the best of life, we must begin by accepting the way it is constituted. We must accept the system as it is and then work within that system, and in terms of that system, to maintain good results and to bring about other desirable results.

When it comes to life itself—unlike human institutions and human systems—it must be accepted as it is constituted, and we must work with it. To work against it, to try to change it from what it is to what it is not, is self-defeating.

God is who He is and the universe is what it is. We must proceed from the authority of God. We must begin with the idea that God really knows what He is doing, more so than we. We must maintain the point of view that, when there is a conflict between our ideas and God's, God's must be right—by definition.

Much of the trouble is our hang-up about God.

It happens for a number of reasons.

Some people have never had any dealings with God to speak of, and so they feel very uncomfortable with the idea. They feel embarrassed and awkward. They can and they must work into it, like learning to speak a new language.

Some people have a harder problem. They are in revolt against some form of human authority—a father, a mother, or a sibling, usually. As a result, they project their anger against all forms and figures of authority that they come in contact with in life. Having had bad experiences with human authority, they will not have anything to do with God, the ultimate figure of authority. They see Him as the embodiment of all they resent and all that they are in revolt against.

Others reject God because of bad experiences they have had with those who profess to be religious and speak in God's name. It must be remembered that religion can be and has been misused and abused. But the same has happened with law, medicine, and science. Men use religion badly, but religion isn't bad. Men serve God badly, but God isn't bad.

Acceptance of God is essential to draw maximum value from life. To stop short of God is to stop short of the Truth and the full benefit of this truth.

Human beings can lead decent and ethical lives without God, but they can lead better lives with God.

The central presence of God in one's life creates a different set of attitudes and conclusions than the absence of God. Each pattern creates a particular style of life.

God's presence makes for maximum happiness, because He provides us with the certainty that is to be found nowhere else in life. He permits us to be free from all other enslavements in human and in non-human form. He protects us against unjust and unfair human power and authority. He makes life with other human beings possible.

Our attitudes influence our actions.

Our attitudes are sometimes all we have control over.

To rebel against life is futile and to resign ourselves to life is deadening.

We must become reconciled to life. We must accept it—all of it. We must work creatively with the material at hand. We must deal affirmatively with the reality of the universe.

<u>Verses</u>

Remember this day. Exodus 113:3

♦ ♦ ♦

The Lord is my strength and song, and He is become my salvation. Exodus 15:2

♦ ♦ ♦

Justice, justice shall you follow, that you may live. Deuteronomy 16:20

♦ ♦ ♦

You shall not follow a multitude to do evil. Exodus 23:2

♦ ♦ ♦

You shall not take vengeance, nor bear any grudge. Leviticus 19:18

♦ ♦ ♦

You shall love your neighbor as yourself: I am the Lord. Leviticus 19:18

♦ ♦ ♦

The judgment is God's. Deuteronomy 1:17

♦ ♦ ♦

You shall hear the small and the great alike. Deuteronomy 1:17

♦ ♦ ♦

You shall love the Lord your God with all your heart, and with all your soul, and with all your might. Deuteronomy 6:5

♦ ♦ ♦

What does the Lord your God require of you, but to…love Him. Deuteronomy 10:12

♦ ♦ ♦

I have set before you life and death, the blessing and the curse; therefore choose life, that you may live, you and your seed. Deuteronomy 30:19

♦ ♦ ♦

And the Lord said: Peace be unto you; fear not; you shall not die. Judges 6:23

♦ ♦ ♦

Direct your hearts unto the Lord, and serve Him only. I Samuel 7:3

♦ ♦ ♦

Turn not aside; for then should you go after vain things which cannot profit nor deliver, for they are vain. I Samuel 12:21

♦ ♦ ♦

Give your servant…an understanding heart…that I may discern between good and evil. I King 3:9

♦ ♦ ♦

Thus has the Lord spoken: "Show mercy and compassion every man to his brother." Zechariah 7:9

♦ ♦ ♦

Love truth and peace. Zechariah 8:19

♦ ♦ ♦

I will give thanks unto the Lord with my whole heart. Psalm 9:2

♦ ♦ ♦

He has dealt bountifully with me. Psalm 13:6

♦ ♦ ♦

I have no good but in You. Psalm 16:2

♦ ♦ ♦

Let them praise the Lord that seek after Him. Psalm 22:27

◆ ◆ ◆

The Lord is my shepherd; I shall not want. Psalm 23:1

◆ ◆ ◆

I will bless the Lord at all times. Psalm 34:2

◆ ◆ ◆

His praise shall continually be in my mouth. Psalm 34:2

◆ ◆ ◆

Keep your tongue from evil, and your lips from speaking guile. Psalm 34:14

◆ ◆ ◆

Forget not yourself because of evildoers. Psalm 37:1

◆ ◆ ◆

Commit your way unto the Lord. Psalm 37:5

◆ ◆ ◆

Cease from anger, and forsake wrath. Psalm 37:8

♦ ♦ ♦

Fret not yourself, it tends only to evil-doing. Psalm 37:8

♦ ♦ ♦

Wait for the Lord, and keep His way. Psalm 37:34

♦ ♦ ♦

Hope in God. Psalm 42:6

♦ ♦ ♦

Let be, and know that I am God. Psalm 46:11

♦ ♦ ♦

A broken and a contrite heart, O God, you will not despise. Psalm 51:19

♦ ♦ ♦

Vain is the help of man. Psalm 60:13

♦ ♦ ♦

Trust in Him at all times. Psalm 62:9

◆   ◆   ◆

Pour out your heart before Him. Psalm 62:9

◆   ◆   ◆

But as for me, I will hope continually. Psalm 71:14

◆   ◆   ◆

This is the gate of the Lord; the righteous shall enter into it. Psalm 118:20

◆   ◆   ◆

Except the Lord build the house, they labor in vain that build it. Psalm 127:1

◆   ◆   ◆

The Lord will accomplish that which concerns me. Psalm 138:8

◆   ◆   ◆

Every day will I bless You. Psalm 145:2

◆   ◆   ◆

Let not kindness and truth forsake you.
Proverbs 3:3

♦ ♦ ♦

Trust in the Lord with all your heart, and lean not upon your own understanding. Proverbs 3:5

♦ ♦ ♦

In all your ways acknowledge Him, and He will direct your paths. Proverbs 3:6

♦ ♦ ♦

For the Lord will be your confidence. Proverbs 3:26

♦ ♦ ♦

Above all that you guard, keep your heart; for out of it are the issues of life. Proverbs 4:23

♦ ♦ ♦

He that is slow to anger is better than the mighty; and he that rules his spirit than he that takes a city. Proverbs 16:32

♦ ♦ ♦

Even a fool, when he holds his peace, is counted wise. Proverbs 17:28

♦ ♦ ♦

But as for me, I would seek unto God, and unto God would I commit my cause. Job 5:8

♦ ♦ ♦

Lay up His words in your heart. Job 22:22

♦ ♦ ♦

Take not heed unto all words that are spoken. Ecclesiastes 7:21

♦ ♦ ♦

This day is holy unto our Lord. Nehemiah 8:10

♦ ♦ ♦

O give thanks unto the Lord, for He is good, for His mercy endures forever. I Chronicles 16:24

17

How I Can Become and Stay Healthy

We have colds, we have accidents, we have serious illnesses, we have weight problems, we have headaches, we have trouble with our nerves, we have trouble relaxing, we are run down, we can't get up enough energy to get through the day.

We see the doctor. He takes care of us. He cures us until this trouble, or some other trouble, starts all over again.

A doctor can do something about what ails you, but he can't do anything about why it ails you in the first place.

There is an unmistakable relationship between our ailments and our actions and attitudes. In all instances? Of course not. In most instances? In more instances than we are willing to admit.

We don't like to admit that we are fat because we are eating our problems rather than dealing with them correctly. We'd prefer to think we suffer from glandular insufficiencies. We don't like to admit that we catch frequent colds so we can stay home or go to bed and thus avoid people and situations we don't want to face. We prefer to think that we are just run down. We don't like to admit that our nervousness is the result of fear, frustration, dissatisfaction. We prefer to blame external conditions rather than internal conditions. We look to internal medicine for inner peace.

Our attitudes and our actions affect our condition. Fear cramps the body; faith relaxes it. Joy infuses the body with energy; a sour disposition drains the body of energy.

Not only do our own actions and attitudes affect our bodies, but we attract and repel individuals and situations by what we are and what we do.

Nobody is interested in a sourpuss except another sourpuss. Nobody is interested in a complainer except another complainer. Nobody is interested in a dissatisfied individual except another dissatisfied individual.

We attract what we are. If we are unattractive in spirit, we will attract others who are unattractive in spirit. If we are attractive in spirit, we will attract others who are attractive in spirit. We are what we attract, and we become what we attract.

A doctor can eliminate our immediate discomfort. But he cannot stop us from repeating the trouble.

Being created in God's image, I share in God's health. God's spirit, which is within me, is a healthy spirit. In observing the spiritual laws of life, I will enjoy life and health; by violating the spiritual laws of life, I abuse life and damage my health.

God's health laws work for me, because I function according to these laws, being a part of God.

<u>Verses</u>

I am the Lord that heals you. Exodus 15:26

◆ ◆ ◆

You shall serve the Lord your God, and He will bless your bread, and your water; and I will take sickness away from the midst of you. Exodus 23:25

◆ ◆ ◆

The Lord will take away from you all sickness. Deuteronomy 7:15

◆ ◆ ◆

I have heard your prayer, I have seen your tears; behold, I will heal you.
II Kings 20:5

◆ ◆ ◆

The Lord will…make strong your bones. Isaiah 58:11

◆　　◆　　◆

A merry heart makes a cheerful countenance; but by sorrow of heart the spirit is broken. Proverbs 15:13

18

The Spiritual Laws of Life and How They Operate

We are surrounded by all kinds of laws:

Physical laws—like the law of gravity, the law of action and reaction, the law of cause and effect.

Economic laws—like the law of supply and demand.

Civic laws—like the laws of the community.

Professional and occupational laws—like the principles of medicine, engineering, music, sports, architecture, printing, farming, merchandizing, salesmanship, business, manufacturing, arts and crafts.

Some of these are man-made laws, but many more are only man-formulated. They are inherent in the nature of things as perceived by man.

We accept the fact that these laws can be made to work for us or against us. The law of gravity keeps us from floating away, and we can go self-confidently about our business. But if we jump off a building, we can get hurt.

Laws are dependable. If we observe them, they work for us; if we violate them, they work against us. If we observe the laws, we are free; if we violate the laws, we become enslaved. If we observe the laws, we succeed; if we violate the laws, we fail. If we observe the laws, we are rewarded; if we violate the laws, we are punished. God, among other things, is a God of Law.

Laws, too, are God's gift to human beings. The fact that the universe operates according to law is evidence that God is constant and dependable. God can be counted on again and again. He is not an arbitrary God who rewards and punishes willy-nilly without rhyme or reason. In fact, He leaves the reward and punishment to us—He offers us the choice of observing or violating His laws. God does not reward or punish—we do, by the choice we make, every time, in every situation.

The laws of the universe are essentially spiritual laws. Since every being is part of this universe, every being and every human being reflects these laws and responds to these laws.

The laws can be observed inwardly and outwardly. They can be arrived at wherever we are and through whatever work we do. These laws can be stated in many ways—from the language of commerce to the language of theology. These laws can be translated from language to language.

The Bible is full of statements reflecting the dependable laws of life.

<u>Verses</u>

You shall therefore keep my statutes, and My ordinances, which if a man do, he shall live by them: I am the Lord. Leviticus 18:5

◆ ◆ ◆

You shall keep My statutes. Leviticus 19:19

◆ ◆ ◆

All the commandments which I command you this day shall you observe to do, that you may live. Deuteronomy 8:1

◆ ◆ ◆

What does the Lord your God require of you but…to walk in all His ways. Deuteronomy 10:12

◆ ◆ ◆

His work is perfect. Deuteronomy 32:4

All His ways are justice. Deuteronomy 32:4

♦ ♦ ♦

If you will walk in My ways…I will lengthen your days. I Kings 3:14

♦ ♦ ♦

The Lord is our Lawgiver. Isaiah 33:22

♦ ♦ ♦

Your own wickedness shall correct you. Jeremiah 2:19

♦ ♦ ♦

Let him that glories, glory in this, that he understands and knows Me, that I am the Lord who exercises mercy, justice and righteousness, in the earth; for in these things I delight, says the Lord. Jeremiah 9:23

♦ ♦ ♦

Seek good, and not evil, that you may live. Amos 5:14

♦ ♦ ♦

As you have done, it shall be done to you. Obadiah 9:15

◆ ◆ ◆

Your dealing shall return upon your own head. Obadiah 9:15

◆ ◆ ◆

In His law does he meditate day and night. Psalm 1:2

◆ ◆ ◆

I have kept the ways of the Lord. Psalm 18:22

◆ ◆ ◆

The law of the Lord is perfect, restoring the soul. Psalm 19:8

◆ ◆ ◆

Show me Your ways, O Lord, teach me Your paths. Psalm 25:4

◆ ◆ ◆

Guide me in Your truth, and teach me. Psalm 25:5

◆ ◆ ◆

All the paths of the Lord are mercy and truth unto such as keep His covenant and His testimonies. Psalm 25:10

◆ ◆ ◆

Teach me Your way, O Lord. Psalm 27:11

◆ ◆ ◆

The law of his God is in his heart. Psalm 37:31

◆ ◆ ◆

Your law is in my inmost parts. Psalm 40:9

◆ ◆ ◆

You render to every man according to his work. Psalm 62:13

◆ ◆ ◆

No good thing will He withhold from them that walk uprightly. Psalm 84:12

◆ ◆ ◆

Happy is the man whom You…teach out of Your law. Psalm 94:12

◆ ◆ ◆

Happy are they that are upright in the way, who walk in the law of the Lord. Psalm 119:1

◆ ◆ ◆

Your law is my delight. Psalm 119:77

◆ ◆ ◆

Oh how love I Your law! It is my meditation all the day. Psalm 119:97

◆ ◆ ◆

He that walks uprightly walks securely. Proverbs 10:9

◆ ◆ ◆

The wages of the righteous is life. Proverbs 10:16

◆ ◆ ◆

The merciful man does good to his own soul; but he that is cruel troubles his own flesh. Proverbs 11:17

◆ ◆ ◆

He that searches for evil, it shall come to him. Proverbs 11:27

◆ ◆ ◆

In all labor there is profit. Proverbs 1423

♦ ♦ ♦

All the ways of a man are clean in his own eyes; but the Lord weighs the spirits.
Proverbs 16:2

♦ ♦ ♦

Commit your works to the Lord and your thoughts shall be established.
Proverbs 16:3

♦ ♦ ♦

Whoso trusts in the Lord, happy is he. Proverbs 16:20

♦ ♦ ♦

Whoso digs a pit shall fall therein. Proverbs 26:27

♦ ♦ ♦

The Lord gave, and the Lord has taken away; blessed be the name of the Lord.
Job 1:20

♦ ♦ ♦

To every thing there is a season, and a time to every purpose under the heaven.
Ecclesiastes 3:1

I...saw under the sun, that the race is not to the swift, nor the battle to the strong. Ecclesiastes 9:11

He that digs a pit shall fall into it. Ecclesiastes 10:8

Cast your bread upon the waters, for you shall find it after many days. Ecclesiastes 11:1

19

How to Feel Safe

Life is unsafe.

We don't know from moment to moment what might hit us.

We may be injured. We may be killed. We may become ill and die. There's not enough insurance in the world to protect us against harm and, ultimately, death.

The only life insurance we really have is God.

God is Spirit, and the Spirit of God is indestructible.

The universe is a reflection of God. It is an expression of God's spirit.

Since every being is an expression of God, since every being is the reflection of God's underlying and invisible spirit, every being is indestructible.

There is that about us that is indestructible. The spiritual basis underlying every atom of our being cannot be destroyed.

We are only transformed. We are translated from one appearance of life to another appearance of life. We go from life to life.

We are created in the image of God. We live within God, we live as part of God, we live in the presence of God at all times and in all circumstances.

This is the reason why we can feel safe. We are part of Life Eternal, because we are part of God who lives eternally.

As we go through the various uncertainties of life, we now have a way of neutralizing our fears.

As we feel unsafe for whatever reason, we can switch to the concept of our spirit living with God in safety and beyond destruction.

Verses

He will not fail you nor forsake you. Deuteronomy 31:6

◆ ◆ ◆

The Lord, He it is that does go before you. Deuteronomy 31:8

◆ ◆ ◆

He will be with you. Deuteronomy 31:8

◆ ◆ ◆

The eternal God is a dwelling-place. Deuteronomy 33:27

◆ ◆ ◆

Be not frightened, neither be dismayed; for the Lord your God is with you whereever you go. Joshua 1:9

◆ ◆ ◆

He will deliver you. I Samuel 7:3

◆ ◆ ◆

He will save us. Isaiah 33:2

◆ ◆ ◆

I the Lord…have kept you. Isaiah 42:6

♦ ♦ ♦

I will preserve you. Isaiah 49:8

♦ ♦ ♦

I am with you, says the Lord, to deliver you. Jeremiah 1:19

♦ ♦ ♦

You, O Lord, are a shield about me. Psalm 3:4

♦ ♦ ♦

You, Lord, make me dwell alone in safety. Psalm 4:9

♦ ♦ ♦

In the Lord have I taken refuge. Psalm 11:1

♦ ♦ ♦

You will not abandon my soul. Psalm 16:10

♦ ♦ ♦

I shall dwell in the house of the Lord forever. Psalm 23:6

◆　◆　◆

He will guide us eternally. Psalm 48:15

◆　◆　◆

Your right hand holds me fast. Psalm 63:9

◆　◆　◆

It is better to take refuge in the Lord than to trust in man. Psalm 118:6

◆　◆　◆

The Lord shall keep you from all evil; he shall keep your soul. Psalm 121:7

20

How I Can Find Peace

There is nothing in the visible world that can give me peace.

The lack of money brings economic concerns; the presence of money cannot really buy peace of mind.

Work has its frustration.

Friends do not always see eye to eye with us.

Even the best of family ties are threatened and broken by death.

Our health is an uncertain thing.

Our survival is challenged every moment.

There are many reasons to be fearful, restless, and insecure.

How does one find peace under such circumstances?

God alone offers us the only genuine peace.

Once we accept God as a Presence in our life, we can also turn to Him for this sense of peace.

The key word is "turn."

There are many circumstances that can destroy our peace of mind.

There are many situations that can throw us out of balance.

When this happens we feel inner turmoil. Some individual or situation has us locked in and we become bound up in an orbit of action and reaction.

There is a spell over us. We cannot break the tie that binds.

Except in one way: God. God can become our escape hatch.

God permits us escape from any situation that has us in its grip. God permits us release from any human being with whom we seem bound up.

At the moment that we let our spirit turn to God and concentrate on Him, we break the chains that bind us and we are free.

We can do this with feelings, thoughts, people, and situations.

We can do this repeatedly, as often as is necessary under all circumstances.

By doing this we can find relief from the most trying of circumstances.

We can gain and regain our composure.

We can achieve an inner peace and thus better face what we must face. It may seem foolish. But it really works.

<u>Verses</u>

The Lord your God gives you rest. Joshua 1:13

◆ ◆ ◆

The mind stayed on You, You keep in perfect peace; because it trusts in You. Isaiah 26:3

◆ ◆ ◆

Let him make peace with Me. Isaiah 27:5

◆ ◆ ◆

In quietness and confidence shall be your strength. Isaiah 30:15

◆ ◆ ◆

The work of righteousness shall be peace. Isaiah 32:7

◆ ◆ ◆

The effect of righteousness (shall be) quietness and confidence forever. Isaiah 32:7

◆ ◆ ◆

In peace will I both lay me down and sleep. Psalm 4:9

21

How I Can Be Abundant

We live in an abundant universe.

We come into life and we encounter a world filled with what we need.

There is air, food, water, shelter, clothing; a civilization presents us with the achievements of generations; countless services are provided for the common life.

We think of God as spirit but we must remember that God's spirit appears in many forms—air, water, food, clothing, shelter and in the shape of other human beings. These are expressions of God, these are instruments of God, these are channels through which He works, these are forms in which He speaks to us, these are ways in which He answers our needs.

God's abundant spirit fills the universe. We are His creatures.

He did not create us without providing fully for our needs. We are entitled, therefore, to the blessings of life, in whatever form they are needed.

We breathe all the air we need. We look at a sunrise and a sunset until we've had our fill. We find satisfaction in work, we find relaxation through rest, we find joy through permitted pleasures.

We often feel a lack but we are more abundant than we realize.

We are continuously involved in the dynamic process of God's Love which is a process of Giving and Receiving.

We receive continuously in many ways. We receive continuously in many forms. These ways and these forms are just different manifestations of God's spirit.

As we become aware of this abundance we stop feeling impoverished and in want. We are the rich children of a giving God.

As we realize this our attitudes and our actions become much more positive. We begin to feel better.

Money and our needs in this area may be seen in the same light.

Money, too, is a spiritual substance. Money is just one of the forms in which God's abundance is manifested.

We must regard money with the same appreciation that we regard food. If we despise it, if we belittle it, if we degrade it, it will not come to us. We attract or repel every form of being by our basic attitude.

As we remove our false attitudes towards money, as we permit it to enter our lives, as we become aware of its presence, as we bless it, and as we give, we shall receive of this substance as well.

As we begin to see our abundance, we become more and more abundant in feeling and in fact.

<u>Verses</u>

The Lord will make you overabundant for good. Deuteronomy 28:11

◆ ◆ ◆

The Lord will open unto you His good treasure. Deuteronomy 28:12

◆ ◆ ◆

Observe therefore the words of this covenant, and do them, that you may make all that you do to prosper. Deuteronomy 29:8

◆ ◆ ◆

My servant shall prosper. Isaiah 52:3

◆ ◆ ◆

In whatsover he does, he shall prosper. Psalm 1:3

◆ ◆ ◆

Ask of Me, and I will give…the ends of the earth for your possession. Psalm 2:8

◆ ◆ ◆

Return, O my soul, unto your rest; for the Lord has dealt bountifully with you. Psalm 116:7

◆ ◆ ◆

If they hearken and serve Him, they shall spend their days in prosperity and their years in pleasure. Job 36:11

◆ ◆ ◆

Every man also to whom God has given riches and wealth…this is the gift of God. Ecclesiastes 5:18

22

How God Is Spirit

What do we mean by spirit?
   We mean something that is indestructible.
   We mean something that cannot be seen.
   We mean something that is the substance of life.
   To consider God is to be driven to the conclusion that God is Spirit.
   Nothing short of this will do.
   Anything concrete is less than God, because any object has limits in Time and Space.
   Anything our senses perceive or our mind conceives is finite, mortal, limited.
   The seen forces us beyond itself to the unseen.
   The material forces us beyond itself to the immaterial.
   The destructible leads us to the indestructible.
   The tangible points to the intangible.
   The finite directs our attention to the infinite.
   Matter speaks to us of energy which can neither be created nor destroyed.
   The foundation of life is Spirit.
   Life is grounded in Spirit.
   Spirit is the underlying reality guaranteeing the world of appearances.
   Without a spiritual basis, the material world would collapse—or, better, there would be no material world in the first place.
   God's Presence, God's Spirit permeates all of Creation.
   God's Presence, God's Spirit manifests itself in many forms.
   God speaks through many instruments of being.
   God's Spirit finds many channels of expression.
   God is everywhere and in all things.
   We grasp Him, but we cannot hold Him.
   We see His back, but we cannot behold His face.

<u>Verses</u>

You saw no manner of form on the day that the Lord spoke unto you.
Deuteronomy 4:15

◆ ◆ ◆

Yes, with my spirit within me have I sought You earnestly. Isaiah 26:9

◆ ◆ ◆

The spirit of the Lord is upon me. Isaiah 61:1

◆ ◆ ◆

Do not I fill heaven and earth? says the Lord. Jeremiah 23:24

◆ ◆ ◆

I will pour out My spirit upon all flesh. Joel 3:1

◆ ◆ ◆

My spirit abides among you; fear not. Haggai 2:5

◆ ◆ ◆

Not by might, nor by power, but by My spirit, says the Lord of hosts.
Zechariah 4:6

♦ ♦ ♦

Into Your hand I commit my spirit. Psalm 31:6

♦ ♦ ♦

Whither shall I go from Your Spirit? or whither shall I flee from your presence? Psalm 139:7

♦ ♦ ♦

The spirit of man is the lamp of the Lord, searching all the inward parts. Proverbs 20:27

♦ ♦ ♦

The spirit of God has made me, and the breath of the Almighty gives me life. Job 33:4

♦ ♦ ♦

The spirit returns unto God who gave it. Ecclesiastes 12:7

23

How Life Is Symbol

Life is metaphor. Life is symbol. Life is revelation.
    The universe is the revelation of God.
    Every being speaks of God. Every human being is a symbol of some truth.
    Revelation is not restricted to time or place.
    Every moment is a moment of revelation. Every place is holy ground.
    God speaks to us through all the forms of being in His universe.
    God addresses us in every encounter with life.
    God is present in all things and He speaks to us through all things. To learn the language of different forms, to penetrate into the heart of each being, to encounter life is to speak with God.
    All things contain the spirit of God.
    Creation is spirit manifested in many forms.
    Creation is a constant, ongoing process, because God is a living God existing in the Eternal Now.
    We must ask of every encounter: What is God saying?
    We must answer every encounter: This, God, is how I serve You with my being.
    We ask: What have I received?
    God asks: What have you given?
    We ask: How has God loved me?
    God asks: How have you loved?

Verses

You cannot see My face, for man shall not see Me and live. Exodus 33:20

♦ ♦ ♦

You shall see My back; but My face shall not be seen. Exodus 33:23

♦ ♦ ♦

Day unto day utters speech. Psalm 19:3

♦ ♦ ♦

Open my eyes, that I may behold wondrous things out of Your law. Psalm 119:18

♦ ♦ ♦

All things are Your servants. Psalm 119:91

♦ ♦ ♦

And when after my skin this is destroyed, then without my flesh shall I see God. Job 19:26

♦ ♦ ♦

Lo, these are but the outskirts of His ways; and how small a whisper is heard of Him! But the thunder of His mighty deeds who can understand? Job 26:14

♦ ♦ ♦

For God speaks in one way, yes, in two, though man perceives it not. Job 33:14

◆ ◆ ◆

Stand still, and consider the wondrous works of God. Job 37:14

◆ ◆ ◆

How great are His signs! Daniel 3:33

◆ ◆ ◆

He works signs and wonders in heaven and in earth. Daniel 6:27

24

How to Do the Right Thing

Right attitude leads to right action. Right action leads to right attitude.

The universe operates according to various laws and we conform to these laws long before we understand them. In fact, we arrive at an understanding of the laws of the universe, because we have lived by these laws and they have been a part of our experience.

Right action is more important than right attitude.

It is more important that I don't jump off a roof, than that I have a thorough understanding of the law of gravity, before I make up my mind as to what I should do.

It is more important that I observe traffic signals, than that I first develop a deep respect for law and order.

It is more important that I give to charity, than that I will wait until I can give properly with the purest and loftiest of motives.

It is more important that I get along with other people, than that I wait to have dealings with them until I have learned to love them.

Actions mold attitudes, as much as attitudes mold actions.

That's why right attitudes and right actions can be legislated.

Laws regulate actions. As these actions are experienced, they form or reform attitudes.

Life itself is a perfect example of this. As we go through the motions of living, encountering the laws of life, we develop our attitudes about life.

Right actions, however, are most effective when coupled with right attitudes.

You give more when you really believe in giving.

You help more when you really believe in helping.

You work more when you really believe in working.

You love more when you really believe in loving.

You achieve fullest satisfaction and you have the greatest impact when right attitudes accompany right actions.

It is best to act wholeheartedly. But when this cannot be done, it is better to act half-heartedly than not at all. A starving man is more interested in the food you offer him than in the way you serve it.

It is better to have laws regulating actions, than to wait until individuals are ready to act from the right motives. It is better to collect taxes than to ask human beings to contribute their fair share voluntarily.

The one conflict that does arise at times is the one between two right actions that create a dilemma of choice. Which virtue do you choose, for instance, Tact or Truth, in dealing with an unpleasant situation?

In such a case, you must make a choice, and accept the virtue and the shortcomings of that choice. When choosing between virtues, choose that virtue which, for you, is the harder virtue.

<u>Verses</u>

You shall surely rebuke your neighbor, and not bear sin because of him. Leviticus 19:17

◆ ◆ ◆

Rise up, take your journey. Deuteronomy 2:24

◆ ◆ ◆

By Him actions are weighed. I Samuel 2:3

◆ ◆ ◆

Cease to do evil; learn to do well. Isaiah 1:16-17

◆ ◆ ◆

Seek justice. Isaiah 1:17

♦ ♦ ♦

Set your house in order. Isaiah 38:1

♦ ♦ ♦

It has been told you, O man, what is good, and what the Lord requires of you: Only to do justly, and to love mercy, and to walk humbly with your God. Micah 6:8

♦ ♦ ♦

Be strong…says the Lord, and work. Haggai 2:4

♦ ♦ ♦

Make Your way straight before my face. Psalm 5:9

♦ ♦ ♦

Depart from evil and do good. Psalm 34:15

♦ ♦ ♦

Trust in the Lord, and do good. Psalm 37:3

♦ ♦ ♦

The righteous deals graciously, and gives. Psalm 37:22

◆ ◆ ◆

Sing unto God. Psalm 68:5

◆ ◆ ◆

Forsake not the work of Your own hands. Psalm 138:8

◆ ◆ ◆

Honor the Lord with your substance. Proverbs 3:9

◆ ◆ ◆

Withhold not good from him to whom it is due, when it is in the power of your hand to do it. Proverbs 3:27

◆ ◆ ◆

Let us choose for us that which is right. Job 34:4

◆ ◆ ◆

Every man should eat and drink, and enjoy pleasure for all his labor, (this) is the gift of God. Ecclesiastes 3:13

◆ ◆ ◆

Whatsoever your hand attains to do by your strength, that do. Ecclesiastes 9:10

◆ ◆ ◆

In the morning sow your seed, and in the evening withhold not your hand; for you know not which shall prosper, whether this or that. Ecclesiastes 11:6

25

How I Am Looking for God and How God Is Looking for Me

We have needs that the visible world cannot satisfy. There is nothing and no one in this world that can meet these needs fully.

We desire security.

We desire love.

We desire understanding.

We desire reassurance.

We desire a sense of meaning and purpose.

We desire justice.

We desire a personal relationship.

These desires are met partially on earth. These desires are met to some degree on earth. But these desires are never totally, fully and unconditionally satisfied on the strictly human level.

The fact that we have these desires, the fact that we feel these needs means that there must be a way of answering and fulfilling these needs.

God provides this answer and this fulfillment.

God represents security, love, understanding, reassurance, meaning, purpose, justice, and personal concern.

We must turn for our fulfillment from the visible world to the invisible world; we must turn from human beings to God.

This is the meaning behind our strange urges and desires. This is how we can answer these needs.

To address ourselves to an invisible God goes against the evidence of our senses; but to do so is to experience God in our lives and to find evidence of our spiritual nature.

Life is so constituted that we are meant to turn from the inadequacies of the visible world to an embrace of God's invisible Being.

By developing this kind of relationship with God, we actually come to develop a much better relationship with other human beings and the world.

As we turn to God, we need no longer glorify human beings and turn them into gods and expect them to act as gods. We need no longer demand of human beings what cannot be expected of them.

We go in search of God because of the limitations of this life; God goes in search of us by imposing these limitations on us.

<u>Verses</u>

You shall find Him, if you search after Him with all your heart and with all your soul. Deuteronomy 4:29

◆ ◆ ◆

We have made lies our refuge. Isaiah 28:15

◆ ◆ ◆

In falsehood have we hid ourselves. Isaiah 28:15

◆ ◆ ◆

When He shall hear, He will answer you. Isaiah 30:19

◆ ◆ ◆

Your eyes shall see your Teacher. Isaiah 30:20

◆ ◆ ◆

Behold your God! Isaiah 40:9

♦ ♦ ♦

Hear, you deaf, and look, you blind, that you may see. Isaiah 42:18

♦ ♦ ♦

I (God) have not spoken in secret. Isaiah 45:19

♦ ♦ ♦

Come near unto Me…from the beginning I have not spoken in secret. Isaiah 48:16

♦ ♦ ♦

You shall see and be radiant. Isaiah 60:5

♦ ♦ ♦

You shall seek me, and find Me, when you shall search for Me with all your heart. Jeremiah 29:13

♦ ♦ ♦

I will be found of you, says the Lord. Jeremiah 29:14

♦ ♦ ♦

Call unto Me, and I will answer you. Jeremiah 33:3

◆ ◆ ◆

It is time to seek the Lord. Hosea 10:12

◆ ◆ ◆

Seek Me, and live. Amos 5:4

◆ ◆ ◆

Return unto Me, says the Lord…and I will return unto you. Zechariah 1:3

◆ ◆ ◆

In the morning will I order my prayer unto You, and will look forward. Psalm 5:4

◆ ◆ ◆

You, Lord, have not forsaken them that seek You. Psalm 9:11

◆ ◆ ◆

The Lord has made Himself known. Psalm 9:17

◆ ◆ ◆

I sought the Lord, and He answered me, and delivered me from all my fears. Psalm 34:5

◆ ◆ ◆

They cried and the Lord heard, and delivered them out of all their troubles. Psalm 34:18

◆ ◆ ◆

My soul thirsts for God, for the living God. Psalm 42:3

◆ ◆ ◆

He shall receive me. Psalm 49:16

◆ ◆ ◆

I will declare what He has done for my soul. Psalm 66:16

◆ ◆ ◆

The hungry soul he has filled with good. Psalm 107:9

◆ ◆ ◆

In the day that I called, You answered me. Psalm 138:3

◆ ◆ ◆

The Lord is nigh unto all them that call upon Him, to all that call upon Him in truth. Psalm 145:18

◆ ◆ ◆

Acquaint now yourself with Him, and be at peace. Job 22:21

◆ ◆ ◆

He that loves silver shall not be satisfied with silver. Ecclesiastes 5:9

◆ ◆ ◆

From the first day that you set your heart to understand, and to humble yourself before your God, your words were heard. Daniel 10:12

◆ ◆ ◆

If you seek Him, He will be found of you. I Chronicles 28:9

26

How I Can Change

We do not like to make changes.

We do not like to go from the known to the unknown.

We are comfortable with the familiar. We are afraid of the unfamiliar.

This may be said, also, of our style of life.

We may know we are miserable. We may know we should change our habits. We may know we should live differently. But we don't.

We continue our pattern of living, because this is the best way we have found of dealing with the daily demands and challenges of life.

The habits have become entrenched. The pattern has become set.

We may have tried to break the pattern on occasion, but this has usually met with failure. And so we stay as we are, because we do not want to fail again.

But what if we know that we should change?

To change successfully, it is necessary to replace what you must give up with something better. It is not possible to stop an undesirable habit without substituting a better habit, that will satisfy the need.

The decision to change can come about gradually or dramatically. We are usually receptive to making a change when we have hit bottom and we are desperate to try anything.

This, of course, is spiritual brinkmanship. You must hope that at this point you really have a better choice before you and that you recognize it. Many dramatic changes for the better, however, come about at just such moments of truth.

Whatever the circumstances of change, it is essential that the individual sees and believes that what will be gained is more desirable than what is being given up.

This recognition might come instantly or gradually, when the right time, the right place, the right attitude, and the right substitute coincide.

Religion, properly practiced and properly presented, is the perfect substitute for many of today's habits that enslave but fail to satisfy.

Too many individuals meet the tensions of life with compulsive drinking, eating and smoking. These do not really help anyone handle the pressures and the problems effectively. These are the opiates into which we escape without relief and without success. Or we pursue pleasure without finding joy, or we pursue power without gaining security, or we pursue work without achieving genuine satisfaction.

We are addicted to gods that cannot still our hunger or quench our thirst. We worship idols that cannot answer our needs. Only spirit can satisfy spirit, only God can feed our souls.

It is never too late to change. Why? Because we are free to choose at every moment, in time and space.

Since God has freedom of choice at every moment in the Eternal Now, we, too, being created in His image and sharing His qualities, are free to choose at every moment of our being.

To break habits may be hard, to change patterns may take work, but it can be done and, given the desire and the conviction, it can be done with dramatic results.

Once we take the first step we are helped along and rewarded in many instant, continuous and unexpected ways.

<u>Verses</u>

And the spirit of the Lord will come mightily upon you and you shall…be turned into another person. I Samuel 10:6

◆ ◆ ◆

God gave him another heart. I Samuel 10:9

◆ ◆ ◆

Sing unto the Lord a new song. Isaiah 42:10

♦ ♦ ♦

I have announced unto you new things from this time, even hidden things which you have not known. Isaiah 48:6

♦ ♦ ♦

For behold, I (God) create new heavens, and a new earth; and the former things shall not be remembered nor come into mind. Isaiah 65:17

♦ ♦ ♦

I will put a new spirit within you. Ezekiel 11:19

♦ ♦ ♦

Make you a new heart and a new spirit. Ezekiel 18:31

♦ ♦ ♦

For I have no pleasure in the death of him that dies, says the Lord God; wherefore turn yourselves, and live. Ezekiel 18:32

♦ ♦ ♦

A new heart will I give you, and a new spirit will I put within you. Ezekiel 36:26

♦ ♦ ♦

He has put a new song in my mouth. Psalm 40:4

♦ ♦ ♦

I shall not die but live, and declare the works of the Lord. Psalm 118:17

♦ ♦ ♦

I considered my ways, and turned my feet unto Your testimonies. Psalm 119:59

♦ ♦ ♦

I had heard of You by the hearing of the ear; but now my eye sees You. Job 42:5

♦ ♦ ♦

Let us search and try our ways, and return to the Lord. Lamentations 3:40

27

How to Stay Joyful

To be joyful is to have a cheerful disposition.

There is no question but that a cheerful, joyful disposition is attractive.

You feel good and you make others feel good. You attract others because they feel good in your presence.

We have all been cheerful at times. We have all experienced moments of joy.

It would be nice, no doubt, to feel this way all the time.

Can this be done? Yes.

How it can be done is really a matter of why it should be done.

Why should we be joyful?

We should be joyful because we have been called into life for a very special and a very wonderful reason—to serve God.

This is a marvelous thing.

Our life has meaning. Our life has purpose. Our life—each life—has a special value to God. We have been called into life to be witnesses for God in whatever way we find to be a channel and an instrument of His Spirit.

To be able to see life in this way is to be able to walk in continuous joy, knowing that we have been chosen to serve no less a Being than God.

What greater honor could have been bestowed on us!

To know God, to walk in His ways, to serve Him, to see His wonders and His miracles in our daily lives, to be conscious of His constant blessings and rewards, to know that we can be His channel and His witness in any place, at any time, under all circumstances is to experience and radiate a spiritual joy that renews itself continually.

Verses

You shall rejoice before the Lord your God. Deuteronomy 12:22

♦ ♦ ♦

You shall rejoice in all the good which the Lord your God has given unto you, and unto your house. Deuteronomy 26:11

♦ ♦ ♦

I rejoice in Your salvation. I Samuel 2:1

♦ ♦ ♦

The Lord God will wipe away tears from off all faces. Isaiah 25:8

♦ ♦ ♦

You shall go out with joy, and be led forth with peace. Isaiah 55:12

♦ ♦ ♦

My soul shall be joyful in my God. Isaiah 61:10

♦ ♦ ♦

Fear not…be glad and rejoice. Joel 2:21

♦ ♦ ♦

You have put gladness in my heart. Psalm 4:8

♦ ♦ ♦

So shall all those that take refuge in You rejoice. Psalm 5:12

♦ ♦ ♦

I will be glad and exult in You. Psalm 9:3

♦ ♦ ♦

I will sing unto the Lord. Psalm 13:6

♦ ♦ ♦

In Your presence is fulness of joy. Psalm 16:11

♦ ♦ ♦

Be glad in the Lord, and rejoice. Psalm 32:11

♦ ♦ ♦

My soul shall be joyful in the Lord; it shall rejoice in His salvation. Psalm 35:9

♦ ♦ ♦

I delight to do Your will, O my God. Psalm 40:9

◆ ◆ ◆

Let all those that Seek You rejoice and be glad in You. Psalm 70:5

◆ ◆ ◆

Serve the Lord with gladness. Psalm 100:2

◆ ◆ ◆

This is the day which the Lord has made; we will rejoice and be glad in it. Psalm 118:24

About the Author

"If I had not been born a Jew," said Rolf Gompertz, "I might have become a Nazi. I was born in Germany."

He and his parents, Oscar and Selma Gompertz, lived through *Kristallnacht*, November 9, 1938, the Night of Broken Glass, dress rehearsal for the Holocaust that followed. They fled to America the following year, when Rolf was 11 years old, and settled in Los Angeles, California. Gompertz returned to Krefeld, his birthplace in the Rhineland, at the invitation of the city in 1987. He was asked back the following year to deliver a 45-minute keynote speech in German on the 50th anniversary of *Kristallnacht*.

Gompertz is the author of eight books, including two biblical novels, *Abraham, The Dreamer/An Erotic and Sacred Love Story*, his most recent, and *My Jewish Brother Jesus*, his first published book, now titled, *A Jewish Novel About Jesus*.

Abraham, the patriarch of three religions–Judaism, Christianity and Islam–is the focal point of *Abraham, the Dreamer: An Erotic and Sacred Love Story*, a fast-paced, provocative, biblical novel, which explores the turbulent love triangle involving Abraham, his emotionally distant wife, Sarah, and her handmaid, Hagar, "the other woman," who is assigned to give Abraham a son and becomes the love of his life.

A Jewish Novel About Jesus, a highly acclaimed biblical novel, was published in 1977 (The Word Doctor Publications) under the title, *My Jewish Brother Jesus*. It deals with the life of Jesus from a Jewish point of view. It was written to set the record straight about the Trial and Crucifixion and, in the author's words, "to create a better understanding between Jews and Christians, so we can live together, side by side, respectful of one another, in dignity and peace."

Other books followed, including *SPARKS OF SPIRIT: How to Find Love & Meaning in Your Life 24 Hours a Day*, a spiritual self-help book; *The Messiah of Midtown Park* (a contemporary play); and *A Celebration of Life* (poetry and prose, including the text of his one-man show). His articles and short stories on Jewish themes, including *Kristallnacht* and his return to Germany, have been published in major newspapers and magazines.

Following high school, Gompertz joined the U.S. Army and served as a German translator in Washington, D.C. He then attended the University of California at Los Angeles (UCLA), where he earned a B.A. and M.A. degree in English literature. He was honored with the Best Student of the Year Award and named a Phi Beta Kappa.

After college, Gompertz worked as an editor of a weekly newspaper in Torrance, California, and then joined the Press and Publicity Department of the National Broadcasting Company (NBC), serving as a publicist and then as a publicity director. He left after 30 years to form his own company, Rolf Gompertz Communications. He has been a UCLA Extension instructor since 1974.

His two books in the field are the highly regarded *Publicity Advice & How-To Handbook* and *Publicity Writing for Television and Film*. (An earlier PR book is now out of print.)

Gompertz, and his family, are long-time members of Adat Ari El, a Conservative synagogue in North Hollywood. He created, produced, wrote and hosted a local cable TV series, *ADAT ARI EL PRESENTS: Journeys into Judaism*, which ran for four-and-a-half years. He has taught adult education workshops and spoken on Jewish spirituality, meditation and mysticism.

He and his wife, Carol, were married in 1957 and live in North Hollywood, California. They have two sons, a daughter, and four grandchildren: Ron & Ouided Gompertz, Neil and Ryan; Nancy & Jonathan Booth, Sean and Michael; and Philip & Linh Gompertz.

Other Books by Rolf Gompertz

ABRAHAM, THE DREAMER
AN EROTIC AND SACRED LOVE STORY
(A Biblical Novel)

This biblical novel offers an intriguing, unconventional and daring interpretation of the life of Abraham, Sarah and Hagar, the "First Family" of Jews, Christians and Muslims.

The biblical text tells us little about Sarah, but the author suggests boldly, as we meet Abraham's wife, that she is a High Priestess serving Inanna, the Sumerian goddess of Love and War. Sarah, who has become accidentally pregnant by her husband, Abraham, orders the child killed, as required of a High Priestess. Reacting emotionally, Abraham revolts against this practice and, in that moment, hears the call of a new, singular, unseen God who tells him to go forth to a new and different land. Ironically, he is also told that he will become the father of a multitude.

Alienated from each other spiritually, emotionally and physically, the childless Sarah offers Abraham her handmaid, Hagar, with whom to have a child, unaware of the attraction that has already developed between the two, culminating in the birth of Ishmael.

When the jealous Sarah gives birth unexpectedly to Isaac, she breaks up the idyllic relationship between Abraham and Hagar, driving the beloved other woman, and her son, Ishmael, away forever.

Abraham has his difficulties trying to understand the will of his new God. In his despair over losing Hagar, he falls back on pagan sacrificial practices, and proceeds to offer Isaac as a burnt-offering, believing that this is what his new God has asked of him. Ultimately, the book asks the difficult question: How can we ever know the will of God with certainty? In the final showdown between Abraham and Sarah, the author offers a surprising and startling answer to this question. (Note: The novel contains sexually explicit material.)

Fast-paced and written with great clarity like his other spiritually themed books, the novel by this Jewish author makes for fascinating, meaningful and, ultimately, inspiring reading.

What others say about 'Abraham, The Dreamer'

"A powerful, modern midrash (commentary) on the life of Abraham, giving it a contemporary ring...The Biblical characters come alive and become very human. It has been meticulously researched and bears the mark of a master storyteller."
—**Rabbi Moshe J. Rothblum of Adat Ari El, a Conservative synagogue in North Hollywood, CA**

"A daring look at the Abraham triangle..., unconventional..., engulfing..., the sexiest, most imaginative account of the lives of Abraham and Sarah that ever has been marketed..."
—**Ari L. Noonan,** *Heritage/Southwest Jewish Press*

"Anyone who wishes to become more familiar with our Biblical ancestors, so as to identify with them and to learn from them and the essential messages of their lives, will be well advised to read the dynamic ABRAHAM, THE DREAMER, which bridges the gap between ancient times and this contemporary moment in which we find ourselves, and explores the profound relationship that links God and humanity in every generation."
—**Allen I. Freehling, Ph.D., D.D., Senior Rabbi (Emeritus), University Synagogue, Los Angeles, CA**

"Simply stunningly brilliant and plausible, in every way...A lovely, powerful and important book."
—**Rev. Alla Renée Bozarth, Ph.D., Episcopal priest, Sandy, Oregon, author of** *The Book of Bliss* **and** *At the Foot of the Mountain*

"It should be noted that this Jewish author uses explicit language in his effort to meld the meanings of spiritual and physical love and how those relate to one's life and worship. I appreciated that, though explicit, I never found it offensive."

—**Carolyn Howard-Johnson, author of the award-winning** *This Is the Place* **and** *Harkening: A Collection of Stories Remembered*

◆ ◆ ◆

A JEWISH NOVEL ABOUT JESUS

This fast-paced novel sheds new light on the story of Jesus and his times. We get to know Jesus the Jew, and his Jewish world. We meet a much more sympathetic Judas, who believes in Jesus but becomes trapped in a deadly political power-play. Meantime, there is seductive Mary Magdalene, who taunts and tempts Judas, but is transformed through him – and Jesus. Yet Pontius Pilate, the Roman procurator, sees Jesus as a greater threat than Barabbas, the violent Zealot leader. Pilate orders Caiaphas, the Jewish High Priest, whose office he controls, to get rid of Jesus. However, Rabbi Gamaliel, head of the Great Sanhedrin, refuses to collaborate with Caiaphas or Rome – he will not deliver Jesus, or any other innocent Jew, to death.

Rolf Gompertz is an observant, practicing Jew, who fled Nazi Germany with his parents. Says he: "I wrote this book as my answer to Hitler, to set the record straight about the pernicious *Christ-killer* charge, which resulted in Jewish persecution for 2000 years, culminating with the Holocaust. I wanted to create understanding between Jews and Christians, so we may live together, side by side, respectful of one another, in dignity and peace."

What others say:

"It is a pleasure to read a description of the trial and ordeal of Jesus from a Jewish perspective."

—**Rabbi Moshe J. Rothblum, Adat Ari El, North Hollywood, CA**

"You write with an easy, fascinating, living style...You kept my interest to the end..."

—Rev. Carl W. Segerhammar, D.D., Past President, Pacific Southwest Synod of the Lutheran Church in America

"I found it very readable...The story was so well told that I wanted to keep on reading..."

—Dr. A. George Downing, Executive Minister American Baptist Churches of the Pacific Southwest

"(A) fine Biblical novel. I was especially intrigued with your suggesting that there was a <u>political Sanhedrin</u> operating in Jerusalem."

—Rabbi Allen I. Freehling, PhD University Synagogue, West Los Angeles, CA

"(The author) has given us a reverent, enjoyable work, and he has reminded us once again, as we need to be reminded, that Jesus and his disciples were Jews..."

—William Sanford Lasor, Professor of Old Testament, Fuller Theological Seminary, Pasadena, California, *The Reformed Journal*, May 1978

"This book...helps us understand Jesus and his inner circle as Jews, with a more sympathetic picture of Judaism than we see in the Gospels."

—Review, *The North American Moravian*, March 1978

SPARKS OF SPIRIT
How to Find Love & Meaning in Your Life 24 Hours a Day
(Personal Development Guide)

Sparks of Spirit refers to truths frozen into words. It contains 27 brief, easy to understand meditations, with a list of supportive biblical verses at the end. As these sparks touch your spirit, they release their power within you, transforming your life, enriching it, and filling it with meaning and love, 24 hours a day.

Sparks of Spirit is a training manual for developing a spiritual point of view, through the use of brief phrases and verses for meditation and soul-conditioning, on a daily basis. The simple, practical system is non-denominational. It can be incorporated into whatever traditional or non-traditional belief system you have. It reflects Western spirituality, based on biblical verses from the Hebrew Bible/Old Testament, shared by Jews and Christians.

Said **Linnda Durré, Ph.D., psychotherapist, author, motivational speaker & TV/Radio Talk Show Host,** "Having always led a successful and productive life, I was very angry, confused, and depressed when I hit a very difficult and frustrating period. The profound writings in your book, *Sparks of Spirit*, were a daily source of inspiration to me and one of the mainstays that led me out of the darkness and back into the light. I knew that God was teaching me lessons, and your book constantly reminded me of His metaphysical wisdom and love. There was and is a reason for everything."

> "*Sparks of Spirit is inspirational, interestingly written, and contains many practical tools for developing and maintaining a useful and happy life.*"
> —**Dr. Norman Vincent Peale, Marble Collegiate Church, New York City, NY**

> "*Many people are troubled these days, and they are searching for ways to find help. Sparks of Spirit may reach their needs and prove to be most helpful to them.*"
> —**Rabbi Aaron M. Wise, Adat Ari El, North Hollywood, CA**

> "*I asked one of our discreet priests to read the manuscript. He advises me that the material is very good and will help many people to relate to the God of Abraham, Isaac and Jacob. He found it good material for meditation and was enthusiastic about your ability to write.*"
> —**Cardinal Timothy Manning, Archbishop of Los Angeles**

> "*In Sparks of Spirit, your thoughts, The Four Noble Truths and the Eightfold Path meet Torah and the Beatitudes—also a little Black Elk and echoes of the reverent religion of the Great Mother of antiquity (and now). You go*

deeply into your own specific tradition and through its integrity you encounter the universal experience of holiness and mystery.

—The Rev. Alla Renée Bozarth, Ph.D., author of *At the Foot of the Mountain* and *All Shall Be Well, All Shall Be One*

◆ ◆ ◆

THE MESSIAH OF MIDTOWN PARK
(Play/Comedy-Drama)

Seventy-seven-year-old Shlomo Hirsch is a harmless, kindly, little old man who quotes Bible verses and sits in a park feeding pigeons. He has known for 50 years that he is the Messiah, but he's never figured out what to do about it. It's worried him lately. After all, he's not getting any younger. Suddenly he thinks of a plan: He will go on a TV talk show and tell his message to the world...

This is a delightful, contemporary comedy-drama about what might happen if the Messiah appeared today. It deals with the complexities and conflicts of our various messianic beliefs, not only within Judaism, but among the major world religions. Whose Messiah can we believe in, all at the same time? The play ends on a surprising note which may very well provide an answer that we can accept, without undermining the various belief systems.

◆ ◆ ◆

A CELEBRATION OF LIFE
(Poetry and Prose)

How do I get through life? What's it all about? That's the question the author asks—for all of us. *A Celebration of Life* takes its title from the author's one-man show, whose full text appears here. In the performance, the author takes his readers (or listeners) on an entertaining, inspirational journey through life, both humorous and serious, in poetry and prose.

The book also features other works, including "The Search: A Song of Man and the Universe," "The Love Song," and other poems from his early and later years, expressing the universal hopes and fears, joys and sorrows of our human condition.

What Others Say:

(Comments about the author's performance of his one-man show, whose text is included in this book and whose title the book bears.)

> *"I want to thank you for a never-to-be forgotten evening. You have something to say and say it well. I know that I and all the others who were privileged to hear you and to see your performance came away from the event feeling great—and that is what it is all about after all. Thank you again for giving of your time, talents and warmth to make a memorable evening for the rest of us. I personally will remember it for a long time to come."*
>
> —**Edith Schlam, Wise Singles, Stephen S. Wise Temple**
>
> *"Your thoughts in poetry and prose evoked many thoughts and memories in all of us. it was a truly delightful evening, one that will not soon be forgotten."*
>
> —**Kimberly Faber, Program Director, Women's International Network**
>
> *"I just called to tell you how much I enjoyed last night's performance. I think it's more than a performance. It's a happening and it's really inspirational. You do a wonderful job of expressing yourself and your life, and you inspire."*
>
> —**Blanche Herring, audience member**
>
> *"Rolf Gompertz offers us a Celebration of Life which is truly that—a show full of life and joy. Something between lecture and performance. Mr. Gompertz's presentation wins our admiration and our affection. He inspires young and older alike to keep plugging when things get rough…and to develop*

their capacities for love. I heartily recommend Mr. Gompertz as an educating entertainer and an entertaining educator."

—**Rabbi Susan Laemmle, Hillel Director/USC, formerly Hillel Director, Los Angeles Valley & Pierce Colleges**

How to Obtain These Books

These books are available as paperbacks from the publisher's online book store at http://www.iUniverse.com or from http://www.amazon.com. The books may be inspected and browsed at either place before ordering. At the web site *select* the *book store* and *search* by *author's name* (Rolf Gompertz) or the particular *book title*. If a title has not been posted yet, it will be shortly. You may also contact the author for more information and updates. Mailto: rolfgompertz@yahoo.com.

0-595-30726-4

CPSIA information can be obtained at www.ICGtesting.com
Printed in the USA
BVOW071207120213

313044BV00003B/306/A